Own Your Wisdom

by Karen Leslie

ISBN: 978-0-9988945-0-8
Own your Wisdom

1. Self-Help   2. Philosophy

Printed in the United States of America
First Printing, 2017

Book Design & Layout:
Design by Lyza Fontana of CreativeHowTo - www.creativehowto.com
Set in Baskerville and Bloem Typeface

Portrait Photos used by permission:
Marci Ralph of Marci Victor Photography - www.marciandvictor.com

Stock Images licensed by:
Shutterstock

Ideas, concepts and advice in this book are not intended as a substitute for psychological counseling. The author and publisher disclaim any responsibility or liability resulting from actions discussed in this book.

Dedication

Dedicated with honor, deep heart love and respect
to the incredible women who continue to inspire
my life and growth!

Table of Contents

Our Wisdom

Our Voice

Our Legacy

Wise Women Awakened

The creation of Wise Women Awakened, a global circle, came from a potent desire to celebrate, honor and unite women in the second half of life for the purpose to share their inspiring life stories, experiences, ambitions, bountiful unlimited passions and defining moments with like-minded soul searchers!

The world is geared for the youth and yet our voices of wisdom need to come to the forefront equally! We are to be valued and respected for our accomplished awakenings, our coming home to our authentic selves, our personal growth and life lessons learned!

Your voice is valuable! You are an ambassador of wisdom and are a part of the portal of compassionate women who have awakened to themselves, their purpose and destinies! This powerful intuitive energy and bond is like a wild fire, moving swiftly across the continents, igniting the world with a beacon of light, hope and love!

"I went into the abyss, wading in my own unknowingness."

Testimony

Change has been a constant companion throughout my life. Thank goodness, because with change comes growth! The woman I have grown to be is not the woman I once was. My journey of self-discovery and wisdom came through deep soul searching, life experiences, and confiding in friends, mentors, and psychologists.

My younger self was always trying to reach a certain level of comfort and security within herself, never being at peace and owning the confidence, *I just recently grew into!*

Along the way, I lost touch with my integrity. While thinking I had arrived, there was something still lacking – a deeper awakening that comes with experience, time, deep inner work and reflection.

I have always tried to better understand myself and with new eyes, knowledge and awareness, I can move forward stronger and wiser to and through the next years of discovery knowing I finally got it – *a feeling like never before!*

Now I have excitement and anticipation of getting to know and portraying myself with the ultimate authentic me I can be! I find people are attracted to that vibration like a magnet. There is a receptiveness without the veils of earlier years of not knowing how I fit in, or feeling invisible to the point of not existing in a healthy way.

I came to realize the powerfulness of the deep knowing that I am finally on the right track of who I was born to be. I have arrived at this beautiful age. I am an ever-evolving woman, a work in progress of learning more and going deeper, as we all do throughout our lives.

I feel a new beginning in my second half of life! I find comfort in the solitude of my wisdom that started in my late fifties, that only I possess – just me – not trying to be someone else. I am grateful to myself that *I have come this far in my personal growth!*

Upon arriving, I decided to let my hair grow into a silver crown of glory! It had taken a year to be able to look into the mirror, not really recognizing myself, from the dark young beauty on the outside, to the bright silver beauty I am now. The glow on the inside was intensified by the silver on the outside and I am finally happy with the transition.

Life is one big transition and this phase is the best so far! As you look in the mirror, be amazed and *own your beauty!*

When ready, I en"courage" any woman to go for the silver! There is a freedom of expression that can't be matched when you are your authentic self through and through! No hiding necessary. Finally, the mask of the old self comes off! Hats off to the new and empowered you!

"It is only when
we change
that people change
around us."

The "Stage" of Change

Choose change, and change will come!

Under the umbrella of my life, my passionate mission is to set the "stage" for change not only in everyday life, in the beauty industry as well!

While honing my craft of 43 years working in the field of cosmetology and non-surgical hair restoration for cancer, burn, alopecia, female pattern baldness and within the client in depth consultation process, I was led through a doorway of mentoring, encouragement and personal growth. As insights and defining moments were presented, I discovered women were hungry to share their stories, experiences and wisdom and as a result created an opening and opportunity for women to look further and deeper than the hair. They got a glimpse into the meaning of what it is to be beautiful, from inside herself!

*By celebrating and honoring the wise
authentic woman, we show how
magnificent this passage of life is,
creating a positive, much-needed
world trend changer!*

The priceless feeling of being comfortable in her own skin, taking this to a whole new level will acknowledge and capture the ageless essence and grace, giving space, sharing with the world that 50, 60, 70 and beyond is timeless beauty and that *"Silver is the new blond, highlighting the light within!"*

As *Agents of Change,* it is important how we present ourselves to the world around us! The energy along with the confidence we exude outside of our homes will attract the people, friends and circle of community desired.

Become conscientious and mindful when dressing and grooming, revealing and expressing your individuality! We need to care about that! By doing so, it shows inner respect gained, as we walk our walk of life. Show up with flair!

It is not about looking younger, it is about who we are deep within ourselves and to demonstrate that fully, whether wearing a flat, or two-inch heel to clothes that represents women in any shape or size. Courageously and collectively we can crumble the walls of assumptions and stereotypes about women, beauty, aging – and in doing so we create the gateway to truth!

From everyday life, to the runway, to gracing the cover on magazines, building and bridging a new community within community and the world, a new brand of heightened evolved beauty... The beauty of wisdom!

Attainable! Realistic! Let the buzz begin!

The Gift of Wisdom

"To

Own your Wisdom

is to

Own your Life."

Welcome to your Wisdom Journey

We are all experts at aging because we are living it!

With all its realizations and revelations, perspectives and perceptions, the consciousness of coming home to ourselves, being in touch with living from our hearts more and recognizing the power of intuition.

As wise women, we are not as driven to the point of exhaustion, we arrive with our sense of self more intact than ever before.

We respect and create healthy boundaries, surround ourselves with people that truly love and care about us. Our vibrational energies are rising and revolving at a higher frequency – clearly and cleanly – which attracts us and is attracted to likeminded people on the same path of awakening to their purpose-filled life.

As long as we are living from our hearts and passions, and listen to our inner voices, we can't go wrong!

With time and trust we can evolve beyond the perimeters of the mind to our greatness!

The birth of our true soul emits such gladness, giddiness with the knowing.

> *Each and every woman*
> *can tap into herself!*

Beyond being friend, mother, wife, sister (even though she is all those things), her true nature is a glorious combination of characters, wearing many hats and masks. Take off those things and she is a magnificent creature!

She is grounded in the wisdom of living inside herself, not from the outside but at last arriving to the comfort of being in her own skin without the drama of life fragmenting and diluting her perfect sense of reality.

The Awakened Woman!

She enjoys the melding of who she is, in a state simplicity.

Simply "being" is a soft melody of the soul.

Acceptance of the grace and gifts that's
been given, the presence of the present
moments, cultivating wisdom through
sacred silence...

Love being on the upswing of life's pendulum!
Keep your glow on!
Live your wisdom!

"Live from the Heart

Live your Passions

Take clues from the Divine

Live and speak your Truth!"

Wisdom Statement

The wealth I have inside me is expanding out to my external wealth life!

Truth!

Now that is a statement! The just-getting-by survival mode of thought is no longer acceptable!

The courage to take this mindset and apply it to our lives is boundless. *I like to keep it real…* and if I can't keep it real with myself, then I am living a fraud not authentic life.

Are we walking in our truth or the fear-based truth? It is a process to self-actualization.

You and I are growing as we climb this mountain of not-just-possibility, but the truth inside us together.

The word *choice* (and ones like it) are being saturated to where we lose and stop owning and living the meaning.

To *choose* an abundant life is to *lose* the power we have to the old tapes in our heads. The lack mentality, not enough worth, my lot in life which has been laid out by our family's, ancestors and yes even friends which by the way we have *allowed* that to influence us until now! Erase and stop pushing re-wind and re-write YOUR VALUABLE story!

The mode of not living your passions are over!

When I write, it is to myself and it is in my growth realizations that I am sharing with all of you because we are all divinely connected and when we collectively stand strong in our "Wisdomhood" the universe will support that high vibration!

So let's begin by resounding together;

Are you ready to be AWAKENED?
Are you ready to be INSPIRED?
Are you ready to OWN YOUR WISDOM?

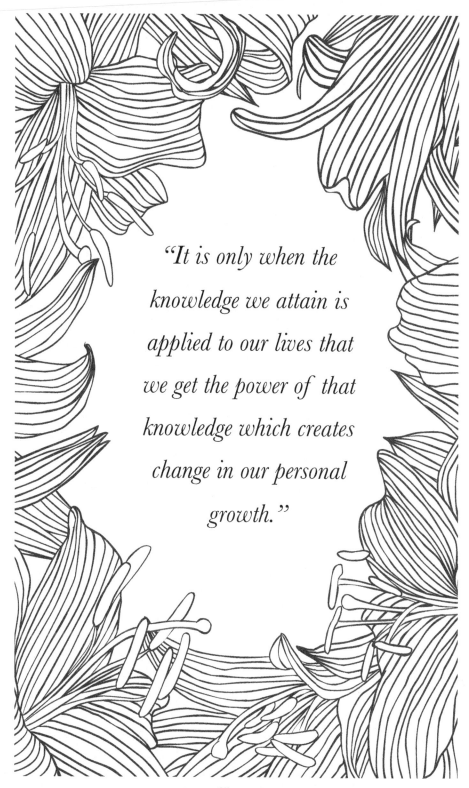

"It is only when the knowledge we attain is applied to our lives that we get the power of that knowledge which creates change in our personal growth."

Wisdomology

The study of wisdom and definitions…

Nature is pure wisdom! Its innate knowing and intuitive vibrational consciousness of what to do and how to grow is ever evolving into the new and does this with sunlight and water.

Our true nature is pure wisdom! This theory is grasped and understood later in life. Our sunlight is knowledge and experience, watering our wisdom with love.

The human circle of life is a constant blooming, withering, and dying process. The blooming is self-growth, as we travel through and to the next phase, old thoughts and patterns wither and die off exposing and allowing our true nature to shine! We become witnesses and observers to the life around us, resetting our hearts intentions, continually letting go and as we shed and step out of our comfort zoned cocoons, like the butterfly, we become vibrant with color and freedom to be our authentic selves!

Wisdom is vast and wide-ranged! From religion to spirituality, a culmination of clarity, integrity, patience, delight, celebration, understanding, flexibility, surrender, abundance and grace.

Wisdom has many definitions in the encyclopedia. Through my research, I am inspired to share the highlights of these definitions that spoke to me, insuring the understanding, breaking down the language barrier, giving clarity of the world of words which is of importance within the context of this book.

WISDOM – the quality or state of being wise, knowledge of what is true or right coupled with just judgment as to action, discernment or incite, in tune with oneself.

WISE – having the power of discerning and judging properly as to what is true or right characterized by showing such power, by scholarly knowledge or learning, to become informed, to instruct, to induce or advise, to show the way, to guide and to direct.

WORTHY – excellence of character or quality as commanding esteem, women of worth, usefulness or importance, as to the world, to a person or for a purpose, your *worth* to the world is inestimable value highly respected, esteemed of commendable excellence or merit, a person worthy to lead.

DESERVE – deservedness: deserving justly or rightly earned, merited qualified for or having a claim to reward, assistance etc… because of ones actions, qualities or situation, worthy of theory that deserves consideration.

Let your genius out of the bottle! Unscripted, empowered, evolved...the infinite you!

Spread your wings and soar!

"*Touch your life,
so you can touch
other lives.*"

Aging Grace

Aging gratefully is the key to aging *gracefully*!

Now is the time in our lives to manifest the true path to our powerful selves, to be a success at it and have a positive outcome. This mentality is a mindset of non-negotiable terms. We cannot get a do over! We have this one life so let's lead it *authentically*!

Knowledge is Your Power!
Take control of the power we all have
been given since our birth.

We all have life stories and sharing in these stories sets us free. It gives us the freedom to be who we are deep within our beings, deep as our wombs.

Let's stay compassionate without judgment as we listen to each other. We all want to be heard and honored, accepted and nourished through our discoveries, and it is through the discovery with others that we see and actually find ourselves. We are like mirrors and reflect what needs to change and grow!

Eye contact is key when building the network of people that you want to draw into your life. Get rid of the riffraff that does not serve you any longer, that zaps your energy. You want to surround yourselves only with people you can relate to and that deeply care about your well-being.

Never ever settle!
Go for the gold always, because the
silver part of our lives is golden!

Women at any age, at the core, are alike in many ways. Yes, we may have had different experiences, but deep down as women, we transcend our essences, beyond the riches, the things, clothes, shoes, jewelry, job, and furniture. These are just things that can be replaced.

YOU are priceless and cannot be replaced or duplicated. YOU are a delicious being, one of a kind like the snowflake and as delicate in emotions.

Let's talk about our homes. As we nest in our home, let's come home to our Authentic selves, home in our hearts and deep in our being.

Get to your core self. Go back to the 3-year-old child inside and be aware of that time when everything was a surprise, was magical, and possible.

We can obtain that wide-eyed-ness again. It takes work, hard work, to honestly take a good look at our selves and know the changes that need to be made – some subtle and some major – but gently we can do it.

Take your life seriously! As adults, I believe we lose touch with the sweetness, the honesty, and the wonder of the birds, the trees, lakes, rivers, oceans, even the moon and the stars. Pause and take time out to notice, not just for a second, but for an hour. Just sit and wonder at our planet and dream.

Do you dream and daydream? Perhaps not, you think you don't have the time but now is the time to do it! Get back in touch with yourself.

Check in with yourself daily and ask these questions:

"Do I have joy in my life?" It's not about the great sale item you just purchased, or the compliment you were given, and have you given joy to others?

"Do I give unselfishly without keeping score?"

"Am I balanced in all areas in my life?" If not, do something about it! Put your armor on, get a warrior mentality and get all that you want and deserve!

"Am I taking care of myself?" Learn how to live an organic, clean, smart life, so you can be an inspiration to not only yourself but to others. Dance to the beat of your best life, yes, like nobody is watching. Watch your life transform as we go into the deeper meaning of your existence.

"How can I be my Authentic self?" Only do what resonates and feels good to you — not what your husband, boyfriend, girlfriend, parents, children, preacher, neighbor thinks that's how you should act, say, or be. One hundred people can tell you: *you look great, you are successful,*

but if you don't feel the deep-down-confidence in your gut and heart, it doesn't mean a thing.

Touch your life
so you can touch other lives!

It is compelling to see the ripple effect of your actions. You are the woman you were meant to be, and in helping and guiding others creates such happiness. If you string a lot of experiences together, you create a tapestry and a bond that cannot be torn or shredded!

Let's keep it simple, let's keep it clean, and let's keep it smart! Our collective intelligence is unstoppable. The strength of a woman, raw like a dog with a bone, don't let go until you feel powerful, unshakable, secure in your wisdom!

Compliment yourself, and believe you can heal your life! Stand powerfully and grounded like a tree. There it is, it can only be done by you, and no one can do it for you even though you wish they could. No more victim mentality! Yes, it tales some major courage.

Take on the Wisdom Mentality!

You are in the best years, and it keeps getting better as we age and continue to grow. If we do the same things every day we get the same results. Change your pattern, drive a different route, take the road less traveled! Life is more interesting and you learn what you are made of.

Fear is the enemy, fear of the unknown, but if you cross over to the unknown, you will get a big surprise! It will surprise you that you meandered successfully and it adds another layer to the fabric of your soul!

Live in gratitude.

Don't just say thank you, but take a deep breath and smell your life and the life around you. If it stinks, air it out with gratitude, honor and respect.

We are all just people, alike, trying to make sense of it all. All of us need each other to encourage our search and transform our will to be our authentic selves. It could be a gentle ride or a bumpy one, but if one can sustain our center without the ripples of life taking us off our growth path, then we can find our inner voice and be on our way to our higher self.

It is a lifetime of work and as rewarding as you "wear a medal of honor in your heart." The heart of the matter is, being comfortable in your own skin. Even a glimpse of that feeling can propel us to new levels of becoming *awakened* to the soul of our purpose here in this lifetime.

Embrace your love and compassion for yourself and others. Watch and experience the richness of the pure heart and feel full and satisfying as a good meal. Enjoy the gift of giving, knowing you are making a difference.

Drink in your life and quench your thirst for self-actualization! Acceptance of the good and the flaws. You wouldn't be who you are today without the suffering of your flaws. The wrong choices show you and teach you not to do it again. Do not keep repeating the things that do not make you happy. Change it up! Keep taking a new approach until you are satisfied with the outcome. Keep saying yes, and try again.

YOU CAN CHANGE YOUR LIFE AT ANYTIME!

YOU choose – life or death. Do not keep living in a dead-end self, YOU can choose and transform yourself anyway you want.

YOU are your own mastermind!

"*Perfection*

is

overrated!"

Imperfection Perfection

The house barely holding itself up...

It breathes through its misfitted screens...

The dribble of the shower head, making its own musical melody...

The primitive drip-drip-drip like a drum beat the kitchen faucet provides...

The floor swaying in its own uneven way...

The majestic mountains are the eyes that keep watch over the dreamers inside...

The owl a hoot serenading its wisdom...

The hush of stillness gently parades over the soul...

Perfection is overrated!

The vintage old character moves the spirit in delight!

The overflow of nature's bounty brings nourishment to the body...

The vast view of ocean brings solitude to the mind...

The heart of the house is the loving kindness energy that radiates through every nook and imperfect cranny...

Home sweet home!

"Simply BEING
is a soft melody of
the Soul."

Sacred Space

Imagine… through creativity and imagination, a space where you can nurture, breathe, decompress and balance your *worthy* self!

There is no place like home! When we simplify, de-clutter, re-arrange and re-design our sacred spaces we actually create our lifestyle!

One cannot live in chaos! The inside of our homes reflect our outer world, the lives we lead. This calls for an action and a positive mindset while investigating the needs and wants in your life. Make it fun!

Want vs. Need.... What are your needs? Your wants? The wants are something we don't need! A positive affirmation! The needs are comfort, housing, car, toilet paper, food and the like, everything else is optional. Take a moment to ponder on which carries the weight of desire. Let go...

As you banter back and forth, sifting and shifting, know this is an important decision making process, of elimination. Yes, eliminate the wants and concentrate on the needs! This will take "nesting" to another level like never before!

When accomplished, every time you walk into your home you will expel an audible *AHHHH, I love my home*! As you simplify you will reveal the extraordinary in your ordinary things!

"*Let go and surrender
to the process of your life.*"

The Letting Go

The letting go is an opportunity for life lessons to be learned and gain deeper wisdom!

The letting go, "the big purge" is the ultimate enlightening experience!

We get weighed down by our stuff, we only think makes us happy.

In reality it stunts our growth!

When purging, we have the opportunity and chance to re-visit memories which are very emotional...

Letting go of the goods will create the opening for more good to come!

A different kind of goodness in the spirit! Who doesn't want more of that?

This act of self-love will give you the life of your dreams and desires...

Other"wise" we remain stuck in the same life and wonder why there isn't change...

When we choose change, change will come!

When questioning any decision in life and things get tough...

My experience is to remember why the decision for change was made...

Stick with it, continue to move forward, stay focused. As women, we feel deeply and get attached to worldly things that somehow defines us when in reality it is like an appendage, encumbering ourselves and growth.

We have a tendency to cover up and hide behind the *things*.

The *things* are meant to enjoy for a while and the *wisdom* is knowing when it is time to let it go so we are able to grow and experience life fully!

Long-term life-altering happiness! It is a feeling that no amount of money can buy!

What comes to mind is a levitation, like the soul literally comes out of the body and the *rich joy* is unprecedented!

Dearest friends, I en"courage" you to visit that place in the heart, to sell or give the things you think you cannot live without and through the giving away and experiencing a person's lighting up who receives it is priceless, and know, by letting go, YOU will live more fully, more *awakened* than before!

It is not the stuff that makes us happy, it is people and experiences that en"rich" us!

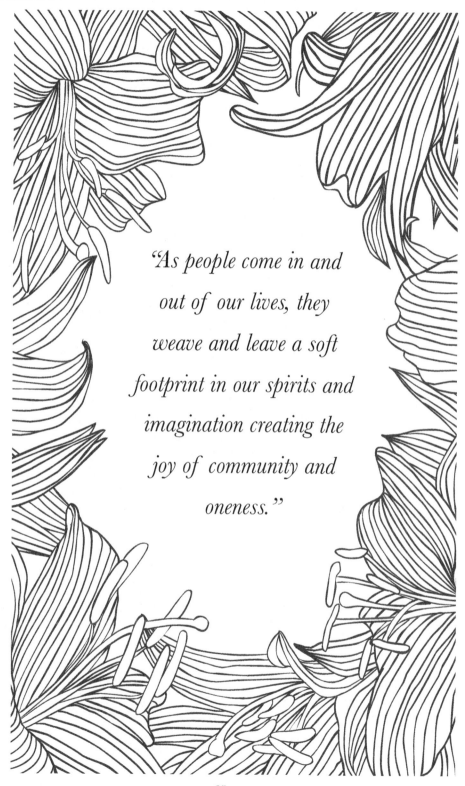

"As people come in and out of our lives, they weave and leave a soft footprint in our spirits and imagination creating the joy of community and oneness."

Footprint

Have you ever taken a moment to look at your own footprint in the sand?

Have you ever thought to step into that footprint, the one that is exclusively yours?

I did exactly that and what I profoundly experienced is... I walked into myself!

The story goes, I was taking a mindful, in the moment beach stroll one stunningly beautiful morning, enjoying the sights and sounds, shells, the texture of sand between my toes, waves soothing me, birds strolling, seagulls crying.

As I started back from where I began, I became involved with patterns from other walks of life, noticing animal prints, tennis shoe prints, barefoot prints of all shapes and sizes, and was stunned to come across my own footprint and pattern in the sand! Fascinated, the imprint showed feet turned out like a ballerina's – narrow and dainty.

Taking a deep breath, I stepped into my own *soulprint*! I felt vibrational grounded energy rise up and through me, something never experienced before!

So, I ask you...

How do you walk through life? What does your energetic footprint say to those around you? Is it light of heart?

Do you hold your head up high with vibrations of love?

Or... do you hold your head down in scattered energy, despair, anxiety, hopelessness or somewhere in between? We all face these moments within our human experience and can assure you myself included!

Walk into your *Wisdom Greatness*, leaving a soft footprint in the sands of life!

"Instant gratification does not give you sustainable happiness."

The Happiness Factor

Sustainable happiness!

Whether one is busy or sitting back enjoying life's view, the important questions are…

- *"Are you happy?"*
- *"Are you doing what inspires you?"*
- *"Do you make a difference in your life and in others?"*

You give your love so generously! Being active in life keeps you young at heart and fulfills your spirit! Let's not leave ourselves out of the equation of the long list of to do's!

The feeling of overwhelm-ness is a signal we are off balance. Be gentle as you weed out what does not serve you any longer.

Instant gratification does not give you sustainable happiness.

What feeds your happiness? What inspires you? There are many variables to sustaining happiness.

Enjoying balance by just BEING instead of DOING, socializing, solitude, creative energy, making jewelry, painting, pottery, writing, dancing, weaving, reading, watching a movie, cooking, visiting with a friend, or simply being content.

As it is inevitable to experience sadness, sorrow, loneliness, fear, grief, and the like – I invite you to embrace and honor these feelings and emotions as well and as we ride these out remember to slip in the joys, passions and dreams in the moments in between, as this helps us to maintain a balance of contented happiness.

When doing so, more and more, closes the gap of the challenging moments, stringing the happy moments closer and closer together, weaving a beautiful tapestry of sustainable happiness! And there it is! In no time, you will discover, experience and playfully celebrate the happiness factor!

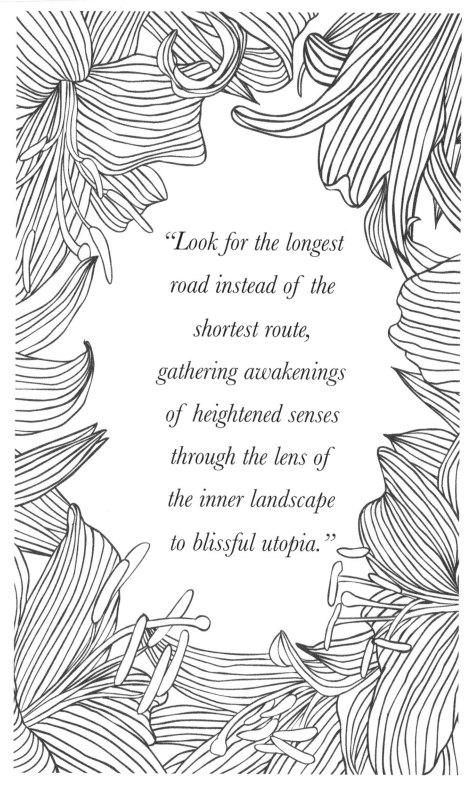

"Look for the longest
road instead of the
shortest route,
gathering awakenings
of heightened senses
through the lens of
the inner landscape
to blissful utopia."

Blissology

Every day can have a blissed-out moment!

What blisses you out?

I often pay attention to the bliss in my life. I believe bliss surpasses, goes beyond joy, in between joy and euphoria.

You feel everything colliding in one moment, love, joy, happiness, anticipation and excitement. I love the fragrance of a rose or wildflowers, the oceans rhythm, the experience of walking into a room, party or event without expectations, the soft unfolding outcome of surprise... priceless!

Blissful moments life offers:

- ♥ A taste of chocolate melting in your mouth
- ♥ An outpouring of joy through creativity
- ♥ Your heart exploding with the happiness of just being alive

♥ The feeling of being in your element

♥ Looking at a newborn

♥ Loving deeply, holding hands

♥ Living your passion

♥ Absorbing being fully in the moment

♥ Feeling the effortless peace within

♥ Could be as soft as a whispering echo in your subconscious, a magnificent sunset or sunrise, a bird calling to its mate or the wind blowing through the trees.

♥ Discover and feel your bliss! It is waiting for you!

"*Wisdom is
Life Lessons Learned.*"

Paths to Wisdom

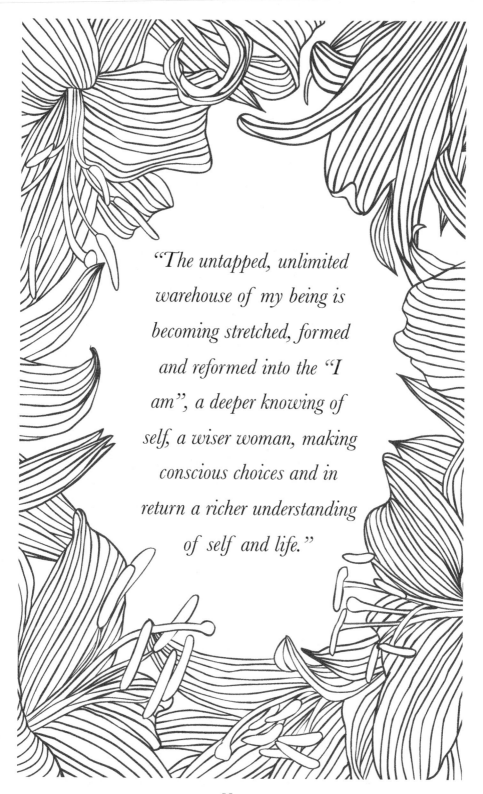

"The untapped, unlimited warehouse of my being is becoming stretched, formed and reformed into the "I am", a deeper knowing of self, a wiser woman, making conscious choices and in return a richer understanding of self and life."

The Power of a Woman's Intuition

If the waters of your soul feel choppy, step back.
Keep testing until your soul's river flows more gently...

Believe and trust in your truth!

If a situation is not resonating, even though there is a trail
of M&M's leading down a path of desire...

Pause and take a scan of the body. When there is anxiety
riding deep in the gut and the scales of self is tipped too
far in the negative... then it is time to circle around your
spirit to find the answers.

Here's to the Power of a Woman's Intuition!

Listen

Honor

Respect

Grow

Grow into the woman you are meant to be, and only be in the presence of people who nurture your soul through-and-through, who listens and responds to your vibrations.

Not just coming from the head, but most precious of all – from the heart!

Balance!

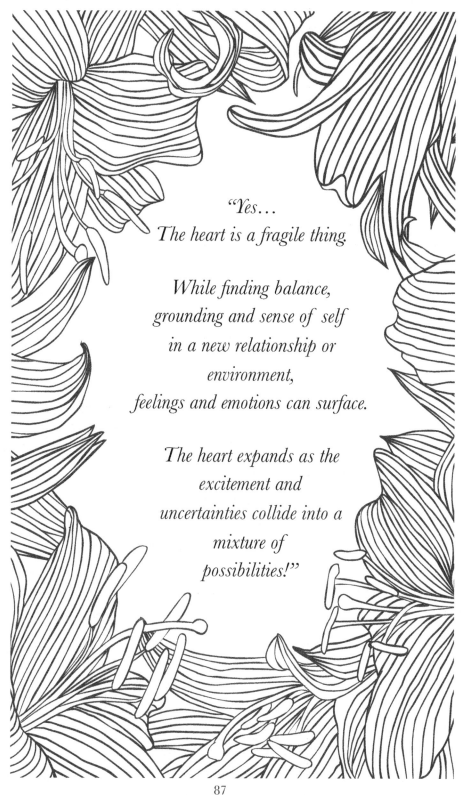

"Yes…
The heart is a fragile thing.

While finding balance,
grounding and sense of self
in a new relationship or
environment,
feelings and emotions can surface.

The heart expands as the
excitement and
uncertainties collide into a
mixture of
possibilities!"

Dance with the Discovery of Self Journey

Notice the delight!

Dial into your vibrational beauty...
Float in the membrane of your human-ness...
Chant your song of the soul...

Like tuning into a radio station, you first hear the static...

The static is: *Not worthy, not enough, alone, isolation, the disconnect, emotional exhaustion, invisible...*

Once fine-tuned you will know your station in life, your life purpose. Yes! most of all your worthy-ness!
In that moment of discovery, re-write your story!

Tune out the old stories of relationships, finance, and friends that do not harmonize with you.

Choose to co-exist within the framework of your values and integrity.

Re-define — narrow it down to the key ingredients that make up who you really are deeply.

Become transparent, vulnerable. Transcend into your Authentic self though and through and watch what happens.

Your world will be changed forever!

Stay centered and grounded within your bubble of security and peace.

The knowing to the depths of your soul that you are not only magnificent… you are capable.

You can steer your own destiny.

Open your imagination and playfully dabble into your deepest desires of the heart.

A woman's heart is ever expanding to the rhythms of nature. Sit quietly to hear your melody. Embrace your love and compassion onto *yourself*.

Be a beacon of hope and love. Once you are lit up with your *Soul Light*, your flame will steadily increase your self-esteem, your every desire and longings will emerge.

From the bottom of my heart, I have experienced this, and I can tell you, your intuitive antenna will pick up the signals of vibrational wishes!

Fine-tune your instrument and get all that you deserve! You are a key player in the bigger picture outside of your circumstances!

Take a walk in God's house, nature's house. That is where you will become connected to the pulse of the earth and to The God within and without to a greater understanding of why you are here...

Simply to love...

Most of all hold yourself like a precious child, a gift...

Remember to greet the dawn each day
with a new knowing of self.

I appreciate your integrity and Authenticity!

Peace to you beautiful ones!
Stay beautiful, inside and out!

*"The Power
is in the Passion
and the Pause."*

Osmosis Bubble

I create a white golden
bubble of self protection
In the most organic
way...

I feel the presence of my
osmosis bubble!

People not on the same energy frequency
Will gently bounce away

Ping...Ping...Ping...

I allow only beings of light
to be welcomed inside my
Loving field!

"To pause is a meditation,
and a vehicle for change."

Yes & No

Say *"Yes"* to your soul-nourishing life!

As women we must preserve our energies.

There are times when life takes us down challenging roads, in many directions, and sometimes all at the same time.

I have come to believe, there are times when we must say *yes* to the "to-do life list" that arises, and equally as important is the word *no*.

One does not need to be busy every minute of the day to be fulfilled. Connecting with the breath of the divine can fill your senses with more delightful depth than that piece of chocolate, Facebook, endless emails, shopping to get more stuff, all filling unmet needs. These things are just temporary.

Instant gratification, unsustainable behavior, temporarily feels good for the moment, and yet cannot compare to the feeling of a happy, joyous, successful balanced life!

By taking downtime for yourself, you are honoring and and taking care of mind, body and heart. This will give strength and clarity to move forward to your highest good! Quiet and solitude is your best resolve. It is a must!

How many responsibilities have you manufactured to please others? How many more times do you want to fall flat on your face in exhaustion or holding your breath for too long creating aches and pains, lack of energy, feeling like you can hardly take another step?

Take control of your out-of-control lifestyle!

Give yourself permission to say *"no"* even if it seems like a good idea. You might not wish to hurt a friends feelings, but what about your feelings?

Are you your own best friend?

As you speak your truth with kindness, breathe easier with the relief of knowing you are taking care of your loving, precious self!

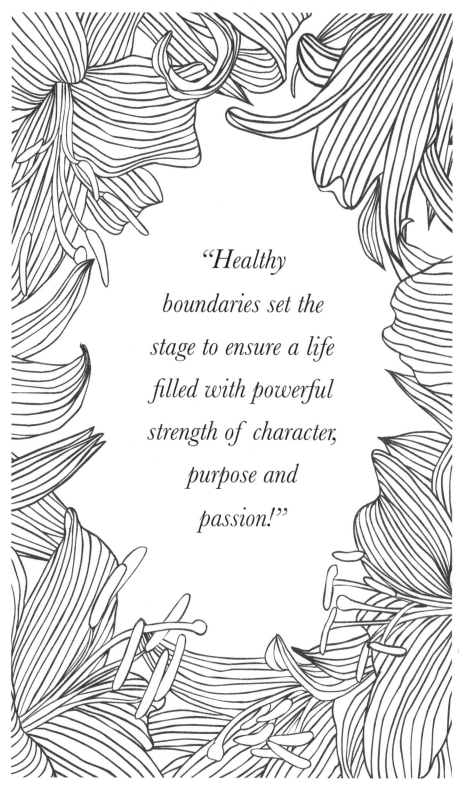

"Healthy boundaries set the stage to ensure a life filled with powerful strength of character, purpose and passion!"

Feed Your Wisdom

*D*ream BIG - Live BIG!

This is at the top of the list of principals to live by.

As women, we sometimes leave ourselves out of the equation of our life purposes and passions. First sit or lay down comfortably (my favorite position) in a quiet, non-disrupted space to listen to your heart. Leave the outside world behind, allow yourself to hear that still small voice that directs you to your highest good and life purpose.

Ask the question: who am I without all the responsibilities and the being-tugged-in-all-directions? Tugged! As you are being pulled by everyone and everything like a puppet on a string, losing yourself in the process, take control and become the golden thread in the tapestry of life by applying your wisdom with authority and confidence!

Try vs. *doing with conviction*! The word *try* has too many holes in your plan of action! A do-it-in-life attitude says complete follow through, commitment, believing you are capable and strong, making room, not getting side tracked and taking you off your path.

You are not a trend or a fad! You come from a long line of warrior women! Honor yourself by shedding the things that no longer serve you, or that steal your joy! Enjoy the security in knowing who you are and not being dictated or defined by how much stuff you have! So, lighten your load! How much jewelry, furniture, shoes do you need?

Choose like-minded and caring friends.

You are a *in-the-moment, evolving woman*! As you empty the heavy trunk loading and weighing you down, you will find a treasure chest filled with your dreams, passions, relationships and community that will take you places you have only dreamed of! Unpack your not-serving-you-now-baggage, and take a trip to your soul! Take the limitations off because the rewards are unlimited!

The term *Knowledge is Power* gives women the personal power in choosing to make decisions that resonates with them on their path, which allows personal growth to emerge! Most of all, be kind and gentle with yourself in the process of re-inventing, re-defining, re-igniting YOU!

Find the sweet spot within your *mindful moments of discovery* and go deeper into your Authentic self and celebrate this passage of life! It just gets better and better as we age and continue to grow! Stay strong and grounded within your self-discoveries and continue to bloom beautifully inside and out!

"It is necessary to
accept before we can
actually love what
is presented."

Rose Colored Glasses

From my youth and throughout my first half of life, I loved wearing my rose colored glasses! My creative heart and dreamer self was colored with the rosy hue, beautifying my ignorance and distorting the facts of life I did not and could not see.

They were a prop, protecting my sensitive heart from struggle and challenge. They kept me from getting blindsided from the curve balls of life that were thrown my way and were a shield to reality. Looking back, the resistance to except the realities of what was, caused much suffering and pain plus wreaked havoc with my spirit, self esteem and value.

With time and wisdom, I have come to realize in the second half of life, there are steps in between to attain and appreciate loving what is. *It is necessary to accept before we can actually love what is presented!* The steps are; accepting the not pleasing situation or relationship, looking at them for what they really are, letting go of what has not worked out and our ideals of what we believe are right and true... and finally comes forgiveness of others and for our actions and choices. The needing to do things my way attitude did not get me very far, and in those times, my rose color glasses deepened to a dark muddy gray. I could not see the way to a peaceful existence and commune with the world around me.

A rocky childhood played a factor in the hiding behind my beautiful glasses, and has taken most of my life to discover the true nature and sequence of being in sync with myself. The illusions dissipated, as I woke up to the importance and value of loving what is, as it is, without ignoring, running away, manipulating, wanting things to be different or trying to change circumstances I had no control over. Big lesson!

I still find I put on my rose colored glasses from time to time with a deeper sense of why. I look through them with new eyes, the eyes of wisdom! I now see the world with a flowy, positive new perspective and grace, accepting what I see in front of me, the colorful beauty of life!

*"Hold yourself
like a precious
child…
A gift."*

Inner Child

Gratitude of where and who you are at this very moment leads to peace, harmony – and less wrinkles!

To be content, happy and thrilled with our life, will create an opening for the veil between this dimension and the unlimited forces that steer dreams, desires and destinies to unfold before our very eyes! Magically!

Think about a child. They believe and trust what they are told. They have a constant expectancy in their hearts and keep asking for what they want, believing they will receive it with innocent in-awe sense of wonder, joy and laughter!

What feeds your inner child?

A butterfly spreading its wings, watching clouds move across a blue sky, fireworks, a picnic in the park, making sand castles, daydreaming, birds in flight, a family of deer, hunting for seashells, walking barefoot in the grass, observing a bee landing on a flower, petting an animal, watching a magic trick, picking wildflowers or just being in the moment watching a sunset.

The simple pleasures that keep our inner child intact and alive is one of the most important, valuable, delightful and freeing part of ourselves! The inner light is at the heart of who we are, just as the laughter of a child fills and expands our spirits!

"*It will always be about the strength of a woman.*"

Woman to Woman

I romanced myself today
With roses and chocolates
Celebrating a milestone of awakening
Awakening to thyself in a whole new understanding
Prepared for my glorious second half of life
Ever more aware of paying attention to the red flags of
life

The knowing of what it feels like to not be in balance
Clarity of the deepest part of me
Paying close attention to what will arrive to me
Relationships coming and going and the ones that
remains

Rooted in my glory like a tree
Arms raised with the strength of release of the unwanted
that does not serve me
Learning more of who I am becoming

And there it is
An ever-learning existence

Knowledge is the deepest part of our center
The heart of the matter

My heart swells and sings with new information
Tapping to the beat

My life is a constant dance of surprises
It will always be about the strength of a woman

The woman I am

"*Live life without borders!*"

Bloom Where you are Planted

There is a saying: *"Bloom where you are planted"*.

But what if you have root rot and need a larger container? Feel like a change is needed? Do you go outside of your circumstances and surroundings?

Take a trip on the inside, meander to your spirit! Why do you have the need to flee your surroundings, the people you love?

For me, it is the terrain. My soul is in the ocean and mountains. What is your spirit telling you? But what is the trade off? Is it worth starting over? Is it an adventure and time to start anew?

Weigh your options carefully. What would be accomplished by transplanting? What would you hope to gain? Is it a better sense of yourself, a sense of fulfillment?

Are you running from yourself and the life you are leading? Or are you going to the life you are meant to lead!

Small changes create the opening
for building upon the
desired lifestyle you crave.

New people, new circumstances could lead to a new beginning or a continuation of the life desired.

In our second half of life, we realize there are consequences to our actions and need to take responsibility. We need to prepare our sense of *self*! Life is an accumulation of our experiences. Your only true guides are your heart and your spirit.

You are not leaving. You are expanding!

"*I am the caretaker of my soul and destiny.*"

The Interior of the Soul Environment

When a tipping point of imbalance happens while in relationship new and old, feeling the shift of weight weighing heavily in the heart...

I find the belly becomes a toxic dumping site! All the unknowns, unclears, uncertainties swim around in this vat of self-doubt and wondering, waiting as the churning raw hope of clarity presents itself....

What's next, I ask???

Move on? OR move in to balance the scales, even out the exchange of goodness!

> *Easing into reflection is a must, to step back, review while taking in the whole!*

Sometimes just a little tweaking of heartfelt communication needs to happen.

The word "Inquiry" is to investigate
without emotion or attachment, and
"Pausing" is the vehicle for change.
To pause is a meditation,
a beautiful beginning.

I am the caretaker of my soul and destiny!

What an *awakening*! All my *darns* are turning into *dreams*!

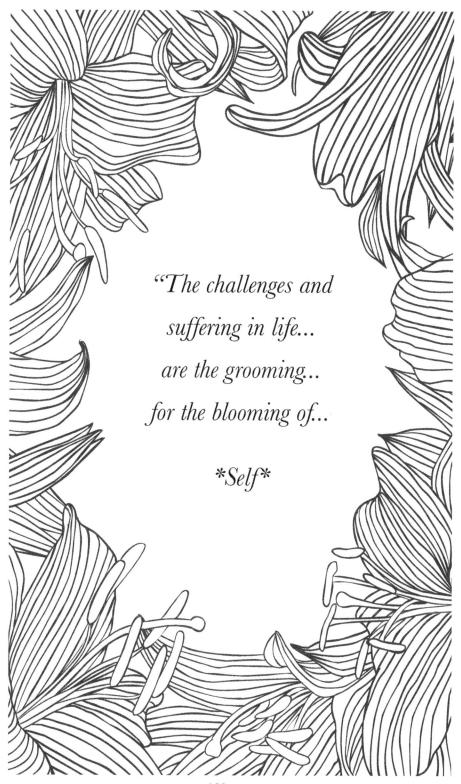

"The challenges and
suffering in life...
are the grooming...
for the blooming of...

Self

Dark Side of the Soul

This story of inspiration came when I was living in Indianapolis, Indiana. I was trying to sell my home and the gray and cold of winter was upon me. The stress of a life-changer, selling all my worldly goods, packing my car with my favorite things, leaving dear friends, community and moving back to my birth home, California.

Things got dark without a light at the end of the tunnel. I got stuck in my thoughts and my life seemed to be on hold. It was a kind of death of the soul moment...

When in transition, those sayings like *"it is all good all the time"* (and the like) are not realistic. We all go through trials, challenges, stress and struggles. Sometimes we are hanging on emotionally by a thread, putting one foot in front of the other, taking the can-hardly-breath shallow breath, living one day at a time even one minute at a time.

I believe that life gets sticky, and the raw truths need to be heard and respected and that we all, each and everyone of us on the planet struggles.

My view on life when I had been struggling to a great degree, (and we all do, if we are honest) that life is not good all the time and those sayings we hear and read to perk us up falls flat in the ying and yang moments when we are in the darkness.

Our life takes on many hues and colors; some muted, some bright. We cannot ignore the fact that everyone of us are on the same path of discovering our palette.

When we come out on the other side – and we always do – there is once again a warm lightness spreading in our spirits!

I believe in the power of positive thought and words because we are writing our future story of how our lives will play out.

And yet...we need to go through these life altering situations to appreciate a deeper understanding... To be in the moment as much as we can, to have gratitude for all the loving people in our lives...

Believe in the power of the Divine and most of all believe in yourself, love yourself even in times of the dark side of the soul!

Live and be your truth!

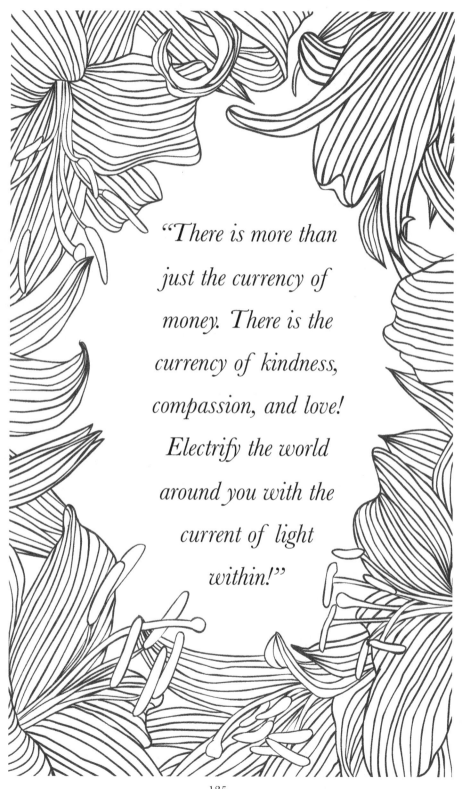

"There is more than just the currency of money. There is the currency of kindness, compassion, and love! Electrify the world around you with the current of light within!"

Tenacity

The tenacity of a surfer...

Hopping on their surfboards...

With solid determination and dedication of the goal...

Fighting the current to master the perfect wave...

Each wave is different yet they persist...

A new wave arises...

The ride is smooth, their spirit soars...

The wave uncurls, crashes too early and down they go...

Courageously they get back up, ride again and again!

A great metaphor of life! Each one of us has that kind of tenacity, as we keep our eyes on the wave of delightful presence of heart!

Undercurrents can take us off our path, yet we continually keep our heads above water, finding the strength to start again, going further than before...

The crashing wave is temporary as long as we stay
grounded and focused on the desired goal...
Fear and resistance can keep us scrambling in the
undercurrent of circumstance...

Pause, take a breath!
Do not drown in indecision!
Remember you are more!
Capable on your path to your personal destiny!

The waves are your passions and dreams...
The undercurrent is questioning decisions made...
Choose not to allow the undercurrents of life to take
you under and off your path of *awakening* to self!
There will always be another wave of opportunity!

At the end of the day, the waters gentle...

The vibrant glow of sunset, bathing you in its light of
love, drenched in spacious completeness of heart,
swelling with the grandness of gratitude for just being
alive!

"*Within
your pain
lies your
purpose.*"

Hope & Uncertainty

Where there is hope...

Comes uncertainty...

Until you ask for what you want or need...

Then leave it to be discovered...

That is when hope turns into and adventure!

Look for the clues and that is...

The Journey

Raw Hope

*H*OPE can be tricky...
There is expectations and a tendency of attachment to
the outcome of the thing you want most at the time...

HOPE can swallow you whole...
You put all your wants, needs, dreams, passions and fears
in one bottle, then when you shake it out and the elated
HOPE you had in your heart is laying on the ground,
with the deep disappointment of the not working out as
you hoped for...

Another *wisdom moment* to be learned!
Your cup is bubbling over with excitement, all you hoped
for and more...

Then...when it collapses and you are stunned into shock
and dismay...

Acceptance needs to come forth...

The letting go of the *almost-oh-so-perfect* situation or relationship is staring back at you with the deep sense of loss in your soul...

What you are left with is a crossroad decision. You can wallow in regret or you can pick yourself back up, brush the dirt off, move forward, start again...

The not-working-out was a blessing in disguise! Something more suited is in your future!

Believe and trust in the process!

Not easy when you feel like you have been run over by a train!

Step back, take a deep breath, call a friend, have a cup of tea...

The universe is smiling down and protecting you! Another opportunity for growth and the *awakening of self!*

"Embrace and celebrate
feeling alive
with harmonic balance
and become one
with your destiny."

The Tantalizing Taste of Life

TASTE the happiness!
As you allow your thoughts to melt away... Drenching
your soul in the moment...
The flavor of exquisite delight becomes palatable...

Round and round we go, on the merry go round of life...
Pluck and taste the flavor of the moment...
Immerse yourself in the texture...
Let it engulf your senses!

Become one with the experience...
As you feel it slide into you...
Feel the deep gratitude of the pleasure it brings...
hmmmm…
Ahhhh…

Hold on and ride out the experience whether it be a good
meal, coming together in community or spending time
with a friend...

NOTICE how everything else falls away except for that single blissful moment in time...

Feeling full and satisfied with the taste of life!

Embrace and celebrate feeling alive with harmonic balance and becoming one with your being!...

Love your life!

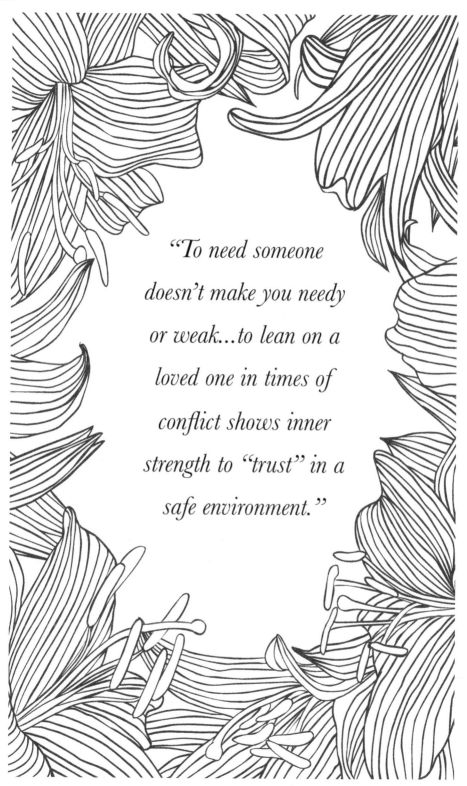

"To need someone doesn't make you needy or weak...to lean on a loved one in times of conflict shows inner strength to "trust" in a safe environment."

Emotional Backbone

Become conscious of your state of consciousness!

Awareness of your environment and existence, sensations and thoughts, inwardly attentive to your state of being is how we gauge and gain perspective to our emotional balance.

Our emotional alignment is important to ensure the stability of life and the passions we hold dear. Misaligned, and the balance is tipped and tension is ripped through our consciousness. It is said, one grain of sand can tip the scales and it is so when pertaining to our souls.

Gaining balance with the feminine and masculine part of ourselves is to visit delicate sensitive patterns. Are you filled with love and compassion or judgment and ridicule? Are you transparent or do you have walls of anger and regret built around you? Are you aware of the tone in your voice? Is it expressed with empathy, softness, understanding, love and kindness? Stay heart connected!

Live life with courage, strength and wonder! Sometimes in our strength we can build a hard shell of protection, close our hearts or cloak ourselves in cold disconnected bitterness even isolate from others. Isolation is the fatality of the soul.

Align with your divine self
and let the beauty shine though!

We need each other even when we are strong! To need someone doesn't make us needy or weak...to lean on a loved one in times of conflict shows inner strength to *trust* in a safe environment!

"Steer Your Own
Destiny."

Tending to Wisdom's Garden

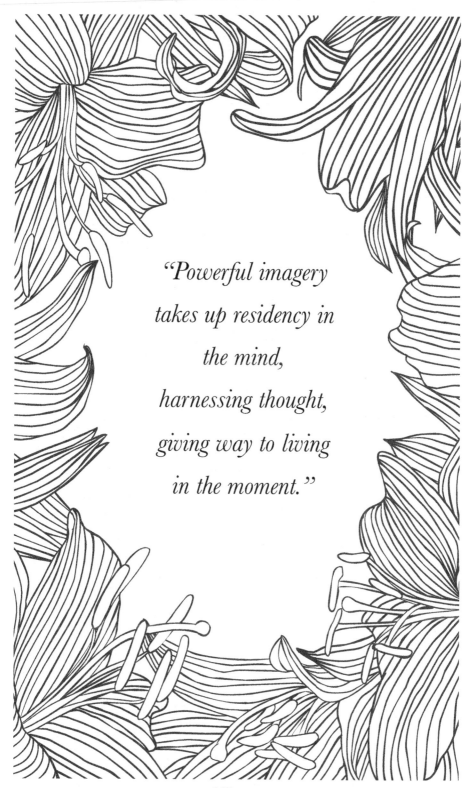

"Powerful imagery
takes up residency in
the mind,
harnessing thought,
giving way to living
in the moment."

Harnessing the Power of Thought

Living in the moment… means letting go of the past and trusting in the future.

To live in each moment we must embrace it, immerse ourselves in it without expectations on ourselves and lives. As we focus and manage our energy, we can then experience, capture and reap the bounty, beauty and wonder of life!

When we rush or hurry we miss and loose the only moment we have, the precious gift of the moment!

Within my practice of living in the moment and the *quiet* in between moments, I find my balance and wisdom, creating the space for new ideas, thoughts, passions and purpose, *easing* into my moments of discovery – a calmness of knowing a conscious existence, a peace and strength, a communing with myself that surpasses all understanding.

Take a moment to close your eyes and just breathe…

Gently visualize the galaxy, see and feel
yourself as a star in the night sky,
suspended, hovering in the vastness of
that moment, not going forward or
backward, up or down, without thought
or memory, time standing still but for
that one moment in time… Powerful
imagery takes up residency in the mind,
harnessing thought, giving way to living
in the moment!

When I am capturing thoughts on paper, I am focused and settled in the moment, not aware of sights or sounds. The hush of awareness becomes alive in my spirit, allowing the Universe to drip its love on me and my life!

Honor your surroundings and the people in your life, taking in the mini moments within each moment, bathing in the human connection on a heart level!

When in the presence of a child, friend, neighbor, loved ones, animals and nature, push the hold button! Let go of wants and needs, the cell phone, Facebook, email, the to do list, spiraling, spinning out with concerns, worry and anxiety of what is next...you are living in the future! Choose an appropriate moment in time for those things! Prioritize your life!

In the present, embrace every moment with a positive optimistic outlook and you will be granted a promising future! Make each moment count! Know you are perfect in this very moment!

We are what we think!
What we think becomes our future so
always be mindful!

The rewards of cultivating the practice of becoming focused, connected with ourselves and thoughts are many! Become an observer of living in your moments, taking notice of the gratitude and peace found while feeling vibrantly alive!... and your life won't pass you by!

A final thought... when it is all said and done, what matters in the end is our relationships, love and respect for humanity, ourselves, the planet, peace on earth and the grace of God!

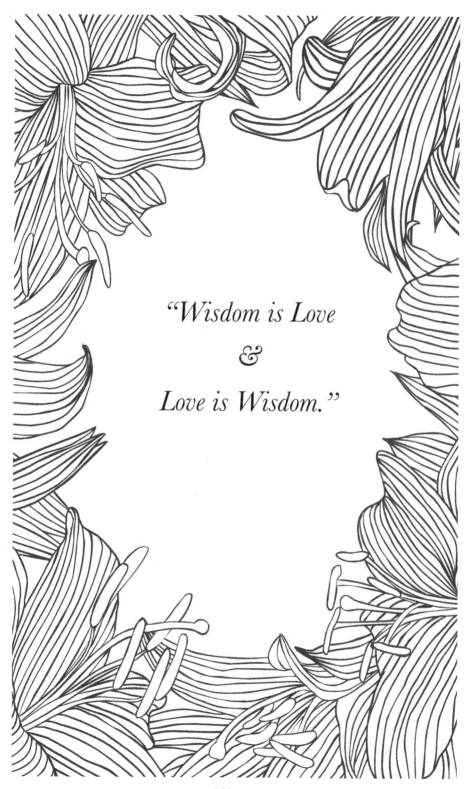

"*Wisdom is Love*

&

Love is Wisdom."

Mindfulness Matters

A restful mind matters...

I am being mindful, thoughtfully dropping into myself, resting in awareness at this moment as I write to you! Meditation, living in the moment, mindfulness are a frothy blend of whipped cream likeness, smoothing out the ruff edges of our thoughts.

There is much to mindfulness, yet it is
as simple as our breath. Gratitude,
generosity, giving ourselves over to our life
and others enhances interconnectedness.

Seizing the quality of the moment prolongs its value rather than seeking quantity of time. You are then able to feel the texture of thought as you savor every moment.

Trust brings wisdom to the body, patience is restorative and healing, non-judging is acceptance, letting go is the release to receive plus non-striving are the doorways to freedom!

In Asia mindfulness and heart-fulness gives wise attention to the soul.

My quest for this topic has opened a gateway to visit the many crystal caverns of my mind, climbing deeper and deeper, traipsing and caving like an archeologist, mindfully exploring, moment by moment, meditatively, gently sweeping and brushing away the debris, all the while re-noticing, re-investigating, re-accepting, re-adjusting, re-discovering, uncovering the treasures that lies inside of myself, honoring and laying claim to my value!

Within my personal sharing.... much showed up while in this process and Odyssey of mindfulness! I noticed in my mind's eye, the self-talk, binging on judgment gobbling up my self-esteem, doubts, challenging my own sense of self and worth, the thought of *"who am I to be writing about mindfulness"* along with other emotions such as accepting what is, even though I want it to be different and the annoyance, frustration, and loss of patience that comes with that mindset! Moving once again into my mind, a rebirthing of wisdom, awareness and growth!

One can visit the past and future from time to time but living there does not give way to expansion!

Simple yet complex when it gets too hard or hurtful and when life gets sticky how we can distract or multitask ourselves into oblivion! If we don't clean up our lives the challenges and pain keeps boomeranging back to us over and over again! A rubber band effect that keeps snapping us to attention of paying attention to the still small voice of the truth, reminding us to follow our hearts!

In this conscious moment of awareness with all our senses intact, ideas, memories, new choices followed by possibilities happen like a comet galloping across the sky to new thought, doing one thing at a time, in time to the music that is only your song to sing!

Live life like it matters!

"When I am planted in my surroundings, my intuitive antenna picks up signals, allowing my instincts to capture the moment."

Nature's Poetry

Nature's influence taps into our natural nature!

I am planting the seeds of my future,
watering them with knowledge, hope and
love. The seeds will bloom and mature
like spring into summer.

Nature's presence is a colorful tapestry of beauty –
weaving and embroidering its wisdom into our eternal
essence of the inner child, playfully and serenely evoking
our senses, inviting us to come fully alive in wonderment!

Nature is our inner guide to our outer wisdom! A
messenger that ribbons itself through and to the cycle of
our lives. Visually stimulating in its offer of splendor,
evoking us to wake up to our authenticity because nature
is ultimately the purest form of authentic powerful
consciousness! Are you conscious of your surroundings or

unconsciously not available to view, absorb and experience the in-awe-ness of its majestic magnificence!

Man's concrete jungle is invading natures privacy!

The universe is moving mountains for us every moment of every day! In trusting, our life becomes a chain reaction of growth, germinating little by little, melding and molding into the grand image of nature's reflection, mirroring back our true nature! Rainbow love!

"I am settled in the bosom of the universe."

The Planet of Choice

The magic of being…being in human form…
Take a moment to unzip your earth suit, crack yourself
open, for just an instant within the infamous beauty of
non-time…

To awaken to the magic, of not just possibility, but the
truth…

The deepest knowing of the embodiment of soul…
The touch of the beyond-ness, fullness, grandness, the
harmonic balancing between the worlds, leaves you in
awe of the what is, and always will be…

The magic of love. The swelling in the heart of bursting
magnificence! The touching, tasting, feeling and hearing
of the angelic embrace to the fiber of your being…

Beyond our thoughts, a resonating with majestic power…
To choose to live within and without of the network
vibration of love, and be hypnotized with the bliss…

Beyond imagination. The grip of truth spins you off your axis, floating in the weightless-ness of pure peace. A glimpse of this sensational awe, and your choices are never the same...

The deep cleansing of the raw and utter thoughts of the what-ifs, will melt away from your conscious, 1-dimension of being, and transform your inner world to the unlimited...

Dance with the angels of the heavens, hold them deep in your heart and burst your *Soul Light* onto the world...
An all-encompassing gold healing bubble that will encapsulate all beings. The unfiltered, undiluted flame will permeate and cast its white light of healing in everyone and in all that there is now and forevermore...

The collective harmonic song of the soul, the OM vibration of love, kindness and compassion, leaves us breathless... connected in the grid of complete-ness...

And so it is...

*"To the God
within and
without,
to a greater
understanding
of why we are
here…
Simply to love!"*

Mass at Dusk in Gods House

The universe at large
A conversation with You.
No mass confusion in God's house
No movement of waters at the lake...
Only the ebb and flow
in God's House in nature's woods

Nature at its best

- soothing - beautiful - classic - rock of ages

This House I see is ageless, beyond forever
Nature at its finest - grandness - peaceful
In awe at the magic of it all

At first glance it is all-picturesque on a grand scale
The music begins, starts out slowly - softly
I become involved in the pictures I see...
The artist's eye, my minds eye takes this scene in
as an artist would paint the Mona Lisa

- perfect - love - life...

The life of the lake animals

The rings of fish feeding on the night's meal

The birds a chatter calling to their mates

The happy bee happily buzzing and dancing with us

Dots of islands on water...

The still of the night...

They unfold grandly from the top to the mirror image of

them...

I see!

I see!

I see God!

Umbrella of Color

Fanning above
The wild blue yonder
Wild with the vast vibrant-ness
Shooting in all directions
The leaves of glory
God's House
Distinctively nature
Naturally beautiful
Yellows so bright
Reds so raw
Ambers a glow
Fires of burning bushes
Autumn leaves start to fall
Fallen on the horizon
Dusk at large
The moon at large
The harvest moon
The depths of its presence
hanging low in its form
It owns the sky
The sky is the limit
In God's House

Winter White

Trees of feathered boas
gracing the yard

Thick froth of snow placed in
the picture without a frame

Taller trees

Tall as the eyes lift up to
the blueness

The slender arms like a
woman's slender wrist with her fingers out stretched and
reaching for answers

This world of winter white

Silenced and hushed except
for the slender white
wrapped arms swaying to the
music of nature

Natures Fence

I look upon the riff-raff of many different leaves of green
They stand sturdy ~ upright in all their glory

Here ~ there ~ everywhere

They build their own fence to gaze upon the visitor in the
yard

They house all the secret creatures of the night ~ yes, the
fireflies ~ the birds

All of Gods special team of nature

Nature a chatter this am

Speaking their own language

With their voices so soothing ~ gently lulling me into this
day

It All is Free

The morning sun will be bright
sky of blue the clouds so white

The ocean breeze, the clouds so high
I gaze upon the birds in flight
In a flock free to roam wings of white
through the sunlight

Oh how I wish I could be so free
To soar the sky
So tired they land upon the warmth of sand

I look around and I see the
beauty of this place I love

I hear the whistling
wind blowing through my mind
I say goodnight till morning light

It all is free
It all is free
It all is free

"*Inspired to be
what already is.*"

Life

ife is a series of prompts.

It's all knowing wisdom softly, gently invites our curious nature, offering a sneak peek into who we really are, exposing opportunities for change, growth, adventure, purpose, passion and love, *awakening* to the truth of ourselves.

It beautifully orchestrates a new direction or action, with its life giving energy, infusing its richness of wonder as its display of beauty captures our imagination giving off sparks of creativity.

Its music is the song of the heart,
a sweet melody of surrender and trust.

A magnificent marathon of senses igniting its wonder and mystery, speaking in its naturesque language, the voice of what is, the anchored force and *power of the light*!

Life is non-judgmental. It only validates our worth.

It sees, hears and rejoices when in balance, blessing us with gifts of life giving waters, the air we breathe, sunshine, rainbows, moonbeams, the milky way and constant unconditional universal love.

We are not alone!
We have everything we need!

Life is continually unfolding, regenerating, re-building, rebirthing, bonding humanity as one.

Holy Mother Earth, I bow down in gratitude for your endurance, patience and forgiveness...

Blessed be Blessed

"Greet the dawn
each day
with a new
knowing of self."

Owning Your Wisdom

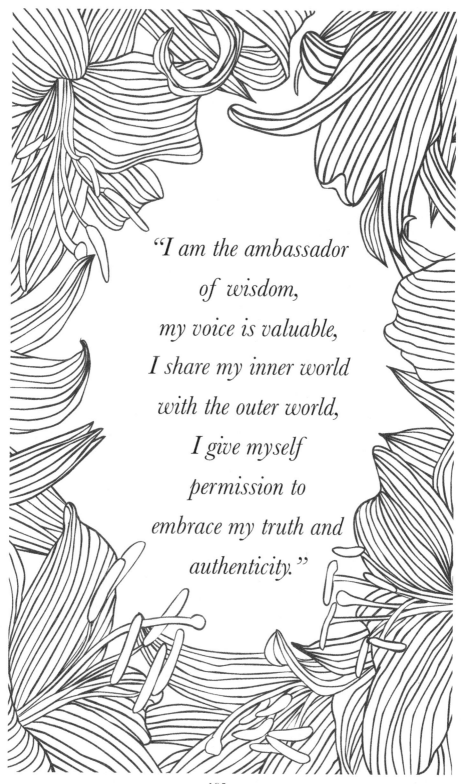

"*I am the ambassador of wisdom,
my voice is valuable,
I share my inner world
with the outer world,
I give myself
permission to
embrace my truth and
authenticity.*"

PhD of Life

Acknowledge and *own* your wisdom! As we conquer our crossroads, our life changes dramatically whether it be from divorce, addiction, family foundations separating and so on; and as our life seems to be deteriorating before our eyes and our emotions are flinging all over the place coupled with the crumbling of self, then...

When we come out on the other side – and we always do – the lessons learned can't be matched as we go deeper into our accomplished selves! The experience is another stepping stone to our strength called *wisdom connection within!*

Own your *PhD of life!* You are certified as a woman determined to continue on to your higher path, valued and deserving self. Saturate, absorb, accept, love, honor, embrace your newfound confidence!

Every woman and each story of life, the challenges, tough decisions, heartbreak brings us closer and closer to our authentic selves.

Wisdom transformed is how we pick up our bruised selves and move forward that counts, not making the same choices we did before. Our eyes are opened to the new way of life we have dreamed for ourselves, to live a healthy, balanced, loving-ourselves-first life. It is only then you will have the *emotional energy* to love others with a new understanding and a compassionate heart. Save that precious resource!

We have just so much emotional strength and we don't want to deplete ourselves for when the important life altering opportunities and choices life presents to us. We then have the knowledge and experience, the backbone, the confidence, the secure-in-our-wisdom attitude to move forward in a new way.

We all fall and stumble and it is within that process that gets us to the other side and our growth. It creates compassion for ourselves and others.

Experience is essential!
It is how we gauge where we were to
where we are at this moment!

Let's celebrate our magnitude of magnificence! What has been accomplished is significant! Don't discount the mountain you just climbed! Be blissful and believe deeply in the fact that this crossroad can be crossed off your to-do list life journey! Wow! Good job! Own it, breathe it, live it!

Your *PhD of Life* mindset is the foundation of your life's work! You earned it! Love that about yourself! Know deep in your soul that these lessons are the part of you that has awakened to your bountiful, unlimited passions and purpose of being – and the result is – *pure confidence!*

You have arrived to your authentic self
through and through.

The ripples of life can't take you off your course so easily. Your unique powerful intuitive energy is valuable!

Tune in and tune up! Speak your truth and witness a lasting change in perceptional wisdom! Feed your state of being with love and speak your truth! Hold sacred space for your triumph's and funky times when lost and uncertain. It is all part of it, the journey to self.

So pack your bags (leaving the old baggage behind) and come with me on a trip to your Authentic self! Your life's medal of honor is in your heart and is carved with glistening healing Love.

Love, it is the song of the heart!

Let's come together and sing the melody of the soul, your eternal essence.

Complete connectedness!

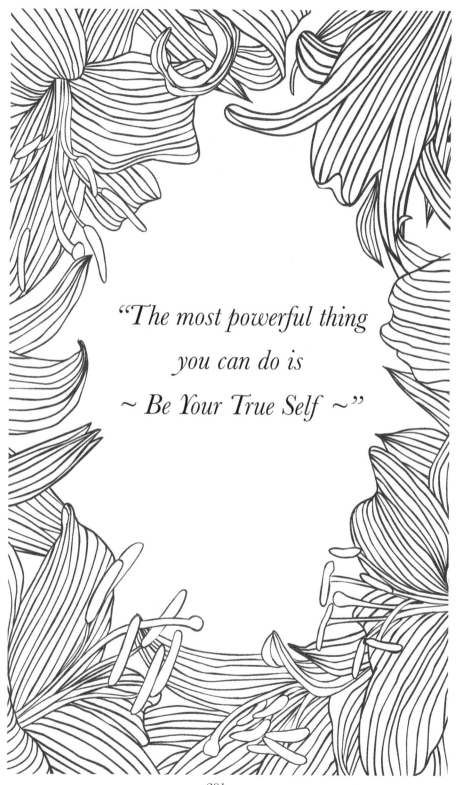

"*The most powerful thing*
you can do is
~ Be Your True Self ~"

Own your Wisdom Creed

To myself first I honor and acknowledge:

To be worthy

To always speak and voice my truth

To feed and own my wisdom

To tap into my intuitive antenna

To be deserving

To be mindful

To be enough

To be comfortable in my own skin

To be capable

To awaken to my bountiful, unlimited passions and
purpose

To be a part of the portal of passionate women to
transcend, transform and delight in our collective
destinies

To co-exist with the framework of my values and
integrity

To be in love with me!

To dial into my vibrational beauty

To embrace love and compassion onto myself

To stay grounded within my bubble of security and peace

To steer my own destiny

To discover and re-write my story

To be a beacon of light, hope and love

To come home to my authentic self and glow from within

To hold myself like a precious child, a gift

To sit quietly and chant my song of the heart

To celebrate and honor my second half of life

To greet the dawn each day with a new knowing of self

To appreciate my integrity and authenticity

To float in the membrane of my human-ness

To be a key player in the bigger picture outside of my circumstances

To stay beautiful inside and out!

To playfully dabble into the deepest desires of my heart

To become connected to the pulse of the earth

To the God within and without to a greater understanding of why we are here...

Simply to love!

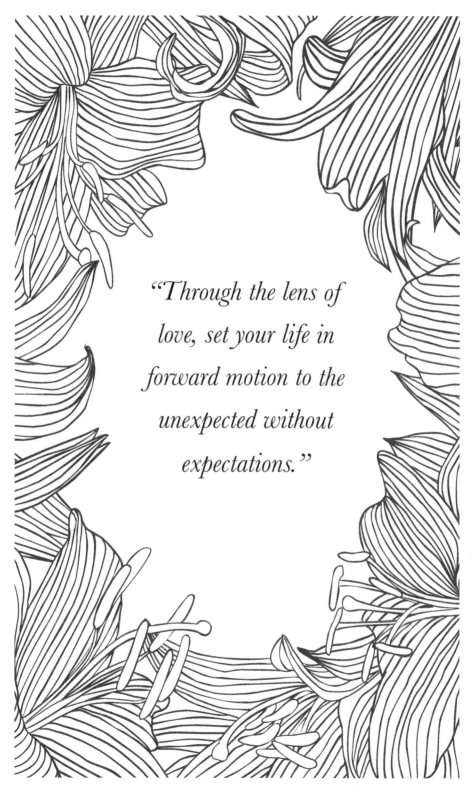

"Through the lens of love, set your life in forward motion to the unexpected without expectations."

Projecting

Life has given me opportunities of late, encountering new relationships, given how fragile my balance is, my path and self can easily get divided...

The getting swept up like the powerful tides of the ocean, the whirlwind of emotions, how quickly I find myself scrambling in the undertow of thought while keeping my footing as it pulls me into the deep murky waters of... I am here again! I thought I learned that lesson!

All of who I am gets a chance to play out the throw of the dice in a new way. Revisiting old patterns!

I am learning and discovering how much I have grown and how many of my old patterns still exists. The *noticing* factor has come into play.

The word for today is *projecting*!

I have caught myself tumbling toward the end of the unfolding, playing out all the details of how it will be...

THE THRILL OF THE RIDE OF EXPECTATION!

Here is where disappointment happens.

Instead, I am:

PRACTICING allowing things to happen, as it happens, organically, enjoying the play of moments by moments as they appear before me.

PAUSING to listen, absorb and witness without my story in the forefront. The stepping aside, letting another person share in my beautiful field of dreams.

HEARING and enjoying their story as they share. I feel sturdier more confident, a comfortable balance of being in my power! I am grateful for the chance to do it differently as I have expanded inward and outward!

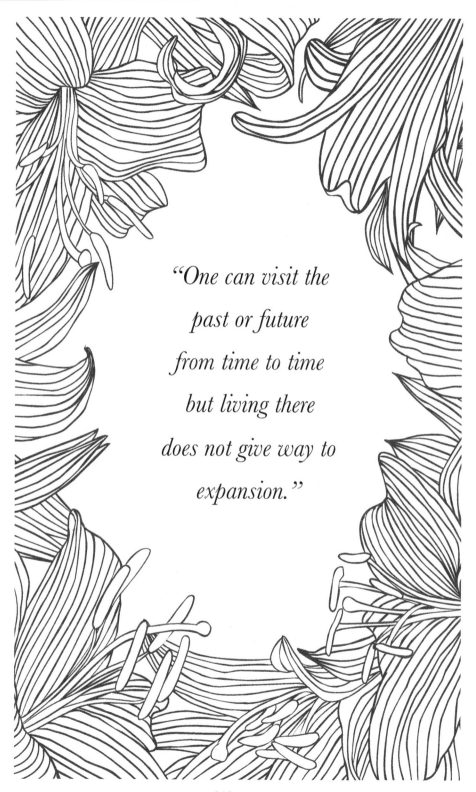

*"One can visit the
past or future
from time to time
but living there
does not give way to
expansion."*

Profound – a Blink of an Eye

The gentle flicker of a light bulb

Light bulb moment

Moment in time

Surprise of pure light

Just seconds of intervals

Blinking quietly

The blink of an eye

Our journey in life is represented to us in that fashion

Blink

Our eyes at birth see the light

Then like the shutter of the camera

Blink - Blink - then blink again

Our lives move along

At a blink of an eye

.

"Honoring your mind,
body and heart
gives strength to move
forward to your
highest good."

Soul Light

As we come to the crossroads and intersections of life.
We are faced with who we are *becoming*.

Life encases and hardens the heart.
Numbs the sense of the soul.

Every one of us is *love* wanting to burst out like a torch.
To shine brightly onto the world!

> *If everything fell away*
> *and you stood there naked*
> *of the drama of life...*
> *Who would you be?*

The answer is your *Soul Light!* Be a beacon in the darkness
of the material world!

Let's come together and talk about our passions, and
living from our *Soul Light*.

All wise women shine brightly, and in doing so, light up everyone around you!

Soul Light represents the expression of
our essence, the light within; our spirit
self apart from our earthly bodies.

Our vibrations are elevated with the confidence of knowing who we are at this incredible intersection in life!

We are honoring our second half of life, crossing over from the girlhood of dreams and fantasies to a pillar of strength!

Quality vs. quantity.

Our choices in what we do, to who we surround ourselves with, changes due to the fact that we realize we have a shelf life! We don't know our expiration date, but we come to realize, the reality that in the not too distant future, we will cross over to that mystical dimension of living purely in our soul essence.

Let's make it count from here on out!

Let's be mindful of what we eat, what we think and what we speak!

Let's choose to eat organic, non-GMO foods to nourish our bodies.

Let's choose to think outside the box, take the road less traveled.

Our thoughts can literally heal our bodies and souls. Toxic thoughts can destroy both.

Let's choose to always speak our truth!

Become confident and comfortable with who you are.

Transcend and come home to your to your *authentic self!*

Stay grounded and centered within your bubble of security and peace.

You are a key player in the bigger picture, outside of your circumstances!

Loving ourselves is the first and most important way to live. We as women tend to nurture everyone but ourselves. Make no mistake, you are worthy and deserve the very best life has to offer!

So go for the silver ring because the second half of life is golden! Own and honor yourself.

There is nobody like you!

You are gifted and make a difference in people's lives! By just being your *authentic self,* the energy and vibration ripples out and felt around the world. The theory of dropping a stone in the pond and watching the rings ripple out is true! That is you!

"Love is the song
of the heart."

Soul Harmony

A circle of Soul Harmony...

A blending of love, heart, heaven and earth...

Gathering gently, filtering toward and through

the circles center...

The beautiful melding of each person...

Like a soft dance through the tapestry of life before us...

Individually facing one another...

With our warm breaths of loving intent...

The singing and blending of each voice...

Weaving through and to the next breath of life...

The soul-filled song...

Like a lullaby of the heart!

Tears trickling down faces from the heart felt intimacy...

Souls bursting and spilling out with joy and love...

Living in the present moment...

In awe of the magical one-ness...

Of the collective human connective-ness...

On a sacred level...

A soaring uplifting of spirit!

"Connect with the
breath of the
Divine."

The Inner Voice

I believe in the integrity of my interior!

My drive and ambition is laying in a puddle of
contentment of just being, putting out the fire of doing.
And yet… there is a niggle in my spirit of a purpose-filled
desire, but not yet louder than being content.
A settling in, not settling for, ordinary!

The drive I had in my 20's, 30's, 40's even 50's to succeed,
I am finding now in my 60's has mellowed.
The battle inside for the what was, to the now is… to
pause and sit with the *"what is"* at this moment is to
honor my self, taking care to not push or wrestle with
what I already know, becoming an observer of thoughts,
and owning my life right here and now! A soft light of
awakening, illuminating the way as I meander on my
journeys pathway.

There is a season when a rest-filled lifestyle is appropriate,
another crossroad to value! It is a settling in of

extraordinary delight of nurturing oneself, a precedent richness of soul, spirit and most of all heart happiness!

"*Trust your inner voice,*
then go out and share it"

A Deep Breath

I am taking a deep breath of the life around me...
My day started out a bit prickly and as I proceeded to
and through the next experience, a joyful bubble of hope
was bursting with anticipation of what was next?
From a nature walk, trimming a woman's hair in the
restroom to sitting with a good friend having coffee and
conversation at one of my favorite places.

I felt a giddiness which I haven't felt in days and hope to
sustain. Yet as I have come to learn and know all too well,
the fluctuation of emotions do vary in different degrees.

Oh, to hold onto the UP moments! To hold on does not leave
room to experience the next influx to another wave of the
new.

As I gaze upon emerald green waters, soothing me in
delight, baring my soul on paper and wondering what I
talk to myself about now? Is it dreams wishing to come
true? Is my wanting so much stopping the Universal

process? To be happy anyway while waiting for them to come true, finding pockets here and there in the in-between moment's, enjoying the picturesque life I have created, is to except the *what-is* at the moment without grasping to the *I-wants!*

To be satisfied with all the gifts that have been given to me and by me on a *silver platter!*

I am in awe with the people that float in and out of my life!

Peak after peak of amazement as the
pieces of my life's puzzle fits together to
create the whole picture — always
expanding into scenes of moving parts!

I surely have up and down moments, sometimes walking around aimlessly wondering...

The question is... *"Where am I going with all this wisdom?"*

The answer is... *"To be continued..."*

"One co-exists within the framework of one's values and integrity."

Collective Wisdom

"Our friendships reflect and mirror our growth and wisdom."

Friendships in the Second Half of Life

In my 60s (not old with my inner child intact), I have experienced my friendships in a new and deeper way. First I have to clarify I did not have many girlfriends, I had boyfriends in my 20s 30s even 40s. It seemed it was all about how I looked and not about who I was.

The focus, commitment, caring, love, respect, honoring, loving me just the way I am, didn't arrive until my late 50s. As I grew (and there is something about the phrase *"Oh grow up!"* that I never liked. It just sounded like I wasn't good enough just the way I was at that moment) and yet, I have grown.

With the girls it was a sort of competition. With the boys I was either a trophy girlfriend or trophy wife. And as far as myself, *it was all about me!*

In the first half of life, we are learning (and by the way, sometimes the hard way!) to what seems to just survive with our dignity intact, focused on just having fun (and sometimes not in a healthy way, you know the partying), our careers – going, going, going - doing, doing, doing - never just being!

In the second half of life,
I feel a slowing down, pausing, reflecting self,
an I-can-breathe-self,
like a slow simmering rush of
a guided response to thought.

We connect more intimately, sensually without the sexuality, with a depth of authenticity and authority over our lives!

We listen actively, absorb and accept. We have learned to respond instead of react (most of the time). We are not on a fast track of life.

We are living our personal passions, dreams knowing what they are in a relaxed manner.

What it comes down to, is our friendships reflect and mirror our growth and wisdom!

We process things differently, our needs change, we are more stable, subtle in our responses. We are patient with ourselves and others. We are not quick to judge because we realize we don't know their life challenges and haven't walked in their shoes.

We have compassionate hearts!
We love deeper!
It is not about looking younger; it is
about who we are deep within.

We have a glimpse into the deeper meaning of what it means to feel and be beautiful. It comes from within and radiates out, not the other way around!

As we present to the world this evolved sense of self, our relationships and friendships become more meaningful, richer, the *you-can-count-on-friendships-when-you-are-down-and-out*, knowing they will be there through thick and thin!

Tuning Fork

Friends are like tuning forks…

- Friends tune and fine tune our wisdom.
- Friends listen, absorb and reflect back the power we already hold.
- Friends meet our challenges, hurts and fears right where we are.
- Friends touch the core of value with the song of sound advice.
- Friends mirror back our deepest truth.
- Friends ring true with chords of vibrational balance.
- Friends tip us right side up when at the tipping point of trapped doubt at the fork in the road.

Friends compassionately hold the chambers of the heart, harnessing the harmony within, embracing us in a loving duet, guiding direction, redirecting us back home, to the woman you already know and are.

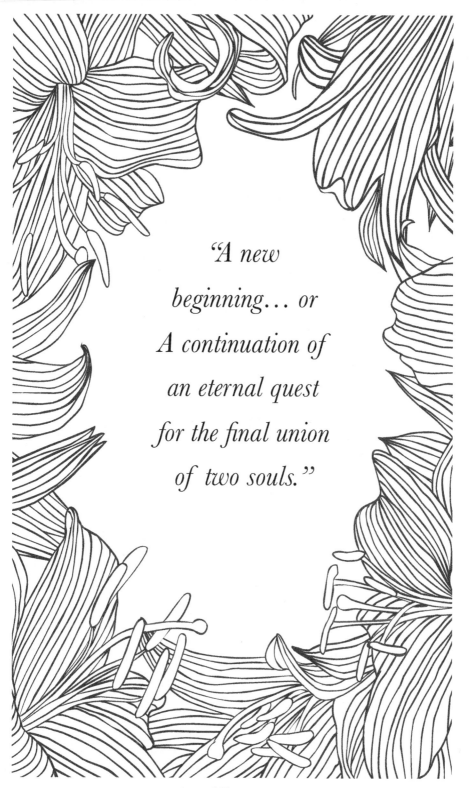

"A new
beginning... or
A continuation of
an eternal quest
for the final union
of two souls."

Bold Love

In our power, we become bold and courageous!

In the showing and asking of needs is a kaleidoscope of openness and freedom to give and receive… a precious gifting of oneself!

The depth of words spoken from one heart to another can take you places richer than all the gems in the world! A diamond in the ruff seas of desired primal longing, diving into the sweet waters of mating with boundless oneness, peering into the *I am* consciousness we all possess.

Unscripted, pure, glorious!

A love affair of the soul, intimately intertwined with another, baths the spirit in the rapture of two bodies expressing the highest form of trust while communicating with touch and breath. The residue is extraordinary!

Bold love is about speaking your truth –
and what your needs and wants are.

Awareness shifts as the walls crumble. Feelings of self-consciousness, such as *I'm-not-enough* or *I'm-not-perfect* dissipate as your glory unfolds – you are found not lost. Floating in wonder and magic of being in the being-ness!

Riding the groundswell of emotions stirred by a soul tethered to another, feels like an entity has permeated and taken up residency in the awakened body, mind and heart. Feeling fully alive, the energy whips up and becomes electric!

Gazing into each others eyes, delving deeply into surrender is like two adults choosing each other, willing to explore while supporting, honoring and free falling together. Desire caresses the senses, breathlessly captivates the imagination, leading to love found in the second half of life!

Boldly believe, your life can be touched… with the possible!

Soul Mingling

The penetration

The gravity pull

The free falling into the abyss of pleasure

The magical mystery

The two souls orbiting within their interior universes

The taste of euphoria

The rush of the pounding tides

The fires lit with every touch

The unexplainable

The powerful plunge of tingling desire

The emotional wonder

The soft gauzy haze of passion

The opening, unfolding, unfurling

The depth of deep beauty

The song of the heart, it's melody resounds and vibrates

through every cell, fully expressing our true nature as

human beings, which is simply,

TO LOVE....

Collective Connection

This story was inspired while sipping coffee in a coffee house...

I became a witness to the comfort of the human connection and the needs of companionship while in a gathering place. And as I observed all walks of life, do what they do, so beautifully I might add, there were various things going on.

From playing solitary games on iPhones, reading, writing, studying or in groups discussing personal or world topics, I felt a bit of sadness and a kind of human disconnect due to technology. On one hand technology takes us to amazing places, connecting us to our world and humankind and on the other hand it sucks us into that little screen for sometimes hours without making eye contact or conversation with another human being even in the same room!

Yet...

There is a comfort knowing we are not alone, doing what fascinates us at the time.

An unspoken knowing...

"Our collective
suffering
is from the fallout
of power and greed,
suffocating our spirits.

Save the planet ~
Save our humanhood"

Humanhood

Heal our hearts ~ heal the world!

Love is our lifeline! The winds of love blows through us all! The wisdom of mankind is as elemental as fire, water, wind, and earth.

The raw organic truth is...
If humans trusted each other like nature
trusts humans there would be an
evolution of peace and oneness.

The human spirit is resilient, strong, vivacious, fiery! We persevere against the steepest of odds! In the rubble of life, we intuitively, spiritually and heart-fully lend the hand of kindness to people in need.

Human beings have the drive and tenacity to see their way through the uncertainties and pain of the world! We rise up from the ashes of our times as phoenixes, shining our inner light onto the darkness of circumstances. We boldly hold the life force of the human spirit like a torch of hope as we adjust, bounce back and recover from change.

To be human is to love, feel and give. The magnitude of our bond of interconnectedness is on a heart and genetic level. *We are wired as one!*

> *When we respect and except each*
> *individual paths, we then become*
> *compatible with humankind, universally*
> *and soulfully united.*

We breathe the same air and walk on the same planet! The survival of our humanity is love and compassion for all beings. Beyond the things we can hold in our hands. We can't buy it or wear it! Faithfully and lovingly, embrace and hold each other and the world in the highest regard.

Our strength, our sacred Humanhood!

"*Honor and lay claim to your Value!*"

Voices of Wisdom

Introduction

The stories of healing, wisdom and defining moments you are about to read are from real women just like you and me. They have come from different backgrounds and with bold honesty, these remarkable women share how they have *sifted* and *shifted* through extraordinary life experiences.

In their personal stories, you may discover a part of yourself, a reflection of the compassionate connection and bond we have to each other. We all stumble and fall along our journey and it is how we pick ourselves up and continue that counts!

As we regain our footing and balance, somewhere deep inside we rediscover our inner strength guiding us to our calling and purpose. We intuitively hear that still small voice that whispers and echoes unconditional love, guiding us to the light of ourselves and letting us know there is more life yet to live!

We have the opportunity to make new choices with fresh visions, clarity and insight to new plateau's with recharged and renewed courage!

Overcoming life's challenges is what makes us who we are and it is in those healing moments we find our...

Voice of wisdom!

"While honoring sadness and grief, let go of the stronghold of control, shake hands with forgiveness and trust, make friends with the unfolding."

Recreate... Reinvent...

By Suzi Wagman

Well I did just that.

I often question whether I have passions. I love my friends, I enjoy my chosen careers, but still inquire of myself if I really have passions. Of course I do, and so do you. What lights us up? What causes our cells to dance...give us the goose bumps? Sometimes it is simply in the moments...

I truly have passion for the isolated moments plus the exhilaration we all get when finding ourselves leaning towards enduring re-invention. Yes?

If I had listened to EVERYTHING my mom (deceased but still advising me) said, I would NOT be where I am today. Bless her loving angel soul... she dispensed a lot of advice so that I would turn out well. I DID turn out well in spite of her (OK, except for a few episodes in there) You see, Mom stressed the need to get a degree and use it. And if you didn't study/get educated for a specific thing, then never mind even considering doing other than that that in life! I used my degree to be employed as a caseworker at the welfare dept. and left there with signs of illness which were merely psychosomatic as it turned out. I got well the day I left!!

SO when the obedient eldest child (me) syndrome collided with the slight rebellion residing in me, I followed an undeniable passion rather than my "degree" and opened a flotation tank center in 1983 with every dollar I had to my name.

Mom thought I was nuts and so did every landlord who I interviewed to rent a space to me and my business partner. Mom said, *"But Suzi, you don't know anything about running a business..you don't have a business degree"*.

Following my passion to open a flotation tank center was certainly a left of center undertaking here in Indianapolis in 1983. It changed my life for the best… connected me to people who are in my life today, led me to my next/ concurrent career… that of a massage therapist.

This profession led me to Thailand to further my study in Thai massage… this snowballed to an innocent side trip to Bali, Indonesia where my love affair with their culture. land, food, spirituality and BATIK FABRIC by the bolt eventually led me to return.

In the USA I did not allow myself the luxury to afford that batik clothing from Bali that I adored. Hark! When in Bali I realized I was immersed in the source for all the fabrics I had previously drooled over!

Wow… I had found the source for this fabric, and amid a culture that I was passionate enough for to spend 36 hours getting over there! A drew my version of a picture on a napkin of a tunic I would like to make, and many details later a career organically unfolded: I began to design clothing and jewelry while in Bali. I am returning for my 23rd trip this year. Yes I had discovered a passion.

"I know, Mom, I never took an adult art class, nor a design class, nor do I know or care that first thing about fashion...what is in/ what is out. God help me!"

I trusted the universe to let my passion win out.

Finding my Way

By Adriana Attento

In his poem Lost, David Wagoner suggests when you are lost in the forest, stand still and listen. *"The forest knows where you are,"* wrote Wagoner. *"You must let it find you."*

You must stop, listen, and breathe.

He's right. One summer afternoon in New York City taught me that when you don't know where you are or where you are going, stand still and listen.

I remember I was working for the automotive industry. It was 1999 and I was depressed and lost. That afternoon I was scheduled to meet a business executive for lunch. We planned on meeting at a deli on the Westside.

I was new to New York and didn't know my way around the streets of Manhattan. As I made my way to the deli, I made a turn, got stuck in traffic, stopped at a light, and then began questioning myself. *"Is this the right way?"*

My grip tightened on the steering wheel. A drop of sweat rolled down my neck. It was hot.

I kept driving and turning and getting stuck in the thick traffic, thinking I could find my way. It was now five minutes to noon. I knew I was going to be late. My grip tightened even more.

In the heat of it all, something inside me said turn left. It was a soft voice, quiet and delicate under the noise of my busy mind. I didn't listen though. I went straight.

After 10 more minutes of stopping at lights and struggling with street traffic, I finally decided to listen to that small inner voice. I went back to the intersection where I had heard, turn left, and I did.

Once I turned, I noticed a department store I had visited once before. And that triggered a memory - the last time I was in that store, the friendly cashier who waited on me struck up a conversation. *"I love to go to the deli around the corner,"* I remember her saying.

And that was all I needed! I knew I was close! I looked again at the address the business executive gave me and within minutes I found the deli!

That day I learned something profound – I could trust my own mind! To my surprise there is wisdom inside, an intelligence that could guide my way! In fact, that afternoon not only did I find my way to the deli, but I also began to find my way in life.

You see, it was then that I began listening to that small inner voice. I started listening to the rhythm inside, to the silent beating forest within. *The forest knows where you are. You must let it find you.*

Being depressed for so long left me disconnected and disoriented in life, which made it difficult to know myself. I doubted myself again and again. But by stopping and listening to the intelligence within, I began to trust. I began to uncover what is true for me, what I like and don't like, what I'm passionate about. I began to peel away what was unimportant and become more and more of who I am. By listening carefully and following that inner wisdom, eventually, I was found.

Many Paths

By Rosanne W

I am not a writer, so bear with me. I have had a unique way of experiencing this thing we call life. I move to a new home, city or state every couple of years. I have been immersed in a variety of flavors, people, landscapes and opportunities. Each brought a blessing and purpose on my journey.

My life is shaped mostly by the different places I have lived and the wonderful souls I have met along the way. Moving was not originally in my blood. I lived in the same house until I graduated college. After college till now, my residences have included the east coast, mid west, west and west coast! I have walked many paths.

What I have learned is *Love God, Love yourself* and *love you neighbor as yourself*. I found happiness. But do you really find happiness? You just know when you do. Close your eyes and feel the blessings around you. You are blessed. Uncover yourself like peeling away the layers of an onion. It can be flaky, transparent and make you cry but your gift is found within. Your gift is shiny and sparkles like a star twinkling in the night sky. How beautiful you are. You possess the beauty of the universe.

You are only on this earth for a short time. Make it wonderful. Become you own best friend, slow down and enjoy the moment and have an open mind. Yes, these are important life lessons indeed.

This wisdom must be experienced in order to truly know it. Soak in the joy, the laughter and the beauty of the world. We all develop our own coping. Don't be in a fog, be mindful of your day. Joy will appear in simple places. Look for it, expect it. Listen to the melodies of the birds singing in nature, look at the bright twinkling of the stars, feel the warm sunshine on your face and begin to embrace *"A simple life well done"*. In a short while, we will all take flight. Their will be more abundant beauty than ever. What is more beautiful than beauty?

A Musical Soul

By Carolyn Bookout

Carolyn Hartman Hughey Bohrloch Bookout has had nine lives in her 82 years. Having a supportive husband of 45 years is a tremendous help with psychological, physical, and emotional well-being.

I knew from an early age that I had always lived and had an inner strength and calmness which helped me make the decisions that made my life. I still use this strength in my relationships from kindergarten on, my daily activities; and any new decisions that I have to make. May this sharing of my life be of some benefit to those searching and learning.

Living on an island ½ mile from Clearwater Beach is the healing climate I desired and discovered on my first trip to Oahu, Hawaii. I played competitive tennis for 33 years with social activities and friendships. Other social clubs, and groups have also been rewarding.

I started my music career at the age of 8 on piano, voice and marimba with six recent performances at Ruth Eckerd Hall with the Clearwater Chorus.

During a performance at one of the High Schools… there was a mystical experience of me seeing all of the people who had helped me from the third grade on… even my parents were in the audience that had passed… all of a sudden I heard the applause and realized that I didn't even know that I had played a single note… this was also a healing of a head and back pain that almost kept me from performing.

My husband and myself will be attending my 65th High School reunion (I have not missed a single one).

Synchronicity

By Linda Lull

When I was young it was a dream of mine to swim with dolphins. I also longed to be a flight attendant and travel and see the world. My first dream of becoming a flight attendant came true in my early twenties, when I found myself flying in Alaska for a commercial airline. I followed my heart and fell in love with a pilot twenty years older than myself. He lived life passionately, and on the edge.

My first powerful precognitive dream was about the airline I was working for – I saw that they would have a deadly crash. When I was in Southern California getting married, the crash that I had feared happened. The morning of my wedding I once again had another powerful precognitive message. This time I heard clearly that I would marry the man I loved, but would be left a widow. This would lead me into a whole new life. This clear message was very unsettling. With the guests arriving, I pushed the message aside and proceeded with the wedding. After ten years of marriage my worst fear was realized when I picked up the phone and was told that my husband had been killed in an airplane crash.

Exhausted and knew it was time to start a start over. An opportunity came to work as a flight attendant for an all first-class airline that flying from Los Angeles to New York. Over time the wear and tear on my physical body started to taking its toll on me. My neck and right arm was in severe pain.

Nothing I did seem to help relieve the pain. By the time I had to stop flying I had lost the use of my right arm. Surgery was needed and I had a very optimistic out look that I would return to work in a short time. Instead, after surgery, my body grew weaker and in more pain with each passing day. The pain medications were not working. Even the everyday simple routines were extremely painful to perform. It was during this time that I prayed to die.

There was a deep inner knowing that if I did not find a reason to live, my life would end very soon.

One day I found myself in a metaphysical book store and saw a flyer to go to Florida with a small group of people and swim with the dolphins. My heart leap at this opportunity. However my logical mind said this did not make financial or physical sense. My heart won out and I signed up for the trip.

The day before leaving I had such a bad migraine headache that I did know how I was going to make the flight? Journaling and looking inside myself I felt that this trip was much more that swimming with dolphins. It was about freedom, unconditional love, trust, and becoming an innocence child again.

My very first swim with the dolphin I was put in a pool with three dolphins and two young boys. The facilitator said that the dolphins usually were more receptive to young child, then females, and then males. With my heart wide open I entered the water and started swimming. The first thing that I noticed was how large the dolphins were compared to me. As they came over to me, I could feel them testing me and eyeing me closely. After some time, all three dolphins started taking turns caressing my body. One dolphin swimming up my front while another dolphin swam down my back. As the session came to a close the only word I could find to describe this experience was *ecstasy*! I knew this was a gift and that I had to let go of expectations of repeating this unique moment. I place this special moment in my heart and knew I would treasure it the rest of my life. As I flew home I wrote down all of the memories and feeling that were arising.

This began a three year journey of connecting with the dolphins in my dreams and in many different parts of the ocean. It also took me on a deep physical, mental, emotional, and spiritual journey of healing.

When I returned home to San Diego something major had shifted in me. My priority was to be with my dolphin friends and restore my health. Even with this new vision my physical body was growing weaker and weaker with each passing day. The medical system did not seem to have any answers other than more surgery. I knew I needed to find a medical doctor that would treat me as a whole person. In Arizona I found a medical doctor that was practicing complementary and alternative medicine. At this point the bone in my neck eight months after surgery had not grafted. I was so toxic that my migraines were a daily occurrence. My doctor said that he was there to assist me on a journey to restore health and balance to my body. I knew that I needed another vision to hold onto. So I shared with him that I was going to swim with the whales.

It has been thirty years since this life changing journey began. This journey has connect me much deeper to Mother Earth and all of life. I say that God gave me the dolphins and whales to be my teachers and this gift saved my life – learning to trust and let go and connect back into that field of unconditional love.

Irish Spirit

By Teresa Donegan

The woman I am today has evolved over the years in personal growth – from tragedies, loss of my wonderful daughter in a scuba diving accident and the tragic loss of my husband soon after in a car accident – helped me to grow in strength and be the woman I AM TODAY.

Growing up in a small village in Clonbullogue Ireland on a farm, having the freedom to run barefoot in the fields and bogs, climbing tall trees in the plantation behind our house, I felt safe to explore the world around me.

In those days with no cell phones, tv or internet, I learned how to do Irish dancing when the neighbors came around in the evenings for entertainment, mastering how to knit so we had warm cloths to wear in the winter, I learned how to sew and read from the light of an oil lamp. Listening to tales about Ghosts and the Banshee. *(The Banshee is a female spirit in Irish mythology who heralds the death of a family member, usually by shrieking or keening. She is often described as disheveled, with long white hair, most often she is seen as an ugly, frightful hag, but she can also appear young an beautiful if she chooses).*

I remember at age 11 years when we got electricity in our wee village, I could walk in a room and turn on a switch, it was amazing.

I gained a lot of strength from my mother, watching her wash clothes in a tub with a washboard for a large family (16), heating water on a stove for the wash, then going outside to hang them on a clothes line, hoping it would not rain until they were dry, (it rains a lot in Ireland).

I am forever grateful to have the modern appliances we have today, so I can continue my relentless quest for knowledge, fun of course, exercising, riding on the back of my friend Rick's Harley motorcycle to the dismay of my daughter Colleen, ballroom dancing, travel and spending time with my wonderful family and friends.

I came to this country in the mid 1960's with nothing more than a caring spirit and a driving ambition to be successful in the world.

I worked to put myself thru Nursing School, while I was raising my wonderful 3 Daughters as a single parent.

Now I am in my seventies, too busy living life to sit in a rocking chair!

Wise Words

By "Di the Wise"

Above all else

we must learn to love ourselves,

take care of our bodies and

cultivate a relationship
with the Divine.

If we do these three things,
we will have lived well!

A Memoire

By Elaine Ferguson

In my favorite memory of my childhood, my brother was about 2 and I was 3. Our dad would put us in a crabapple tree in our yard and go inside to help mom with the dishes. We were too small to get down out of the tree, but could spend hours climbing around in its branches or just sitting on them viewing our world from our exalted position. Years later, after my brother climbed the corporate ladder and I still climbed trees and scaffolding too. Once I told this story to a boyfriend, and his comment was, *"Are you sure your folks were just doing the dishes?"*

When I was 11, I had to buy all my school clothes with the 25¢ an hour I earned babysitting. So I learned to sew. Patterns were 25¢ so I decided I could make my own. My first project was a yellow 'scarf blouse.' It had triangular sleeves and a scarf collar. I had no idea at that time that I was teaching my brain to design in two dimensions something that would be in three dimensions, a skill I would put to good use designing houses.

I was sent to college to get my Mrs. It took two years. My husband decreed *"no kids and no pets!"* Twenty years later, after three kids and numerous pets I managed to escape that abusive marriage. I worked selling World Book Encyclopedia door to door, and did quite well, after my manager convinced me I was smart (not a "stupid, illogical woman"). I learned to talk to people without fear of appearing stupid.

I left him for a penniless older man who treasured me, made me think I had value. So I grew. My dream man had been someone who would tell me what to do, to think, and to believe so I didn't have to make decisions. Instead, my new husband needed me to tell him those things. So I grew. I discovered I could make god decisions. I was good at planning and organizing. Because he was a contractor I channeled my love of art into designing houses, making it a 35-year career.

After many happy years of ballroom and square dancing, traveling and building together, my husband had a stroke. I found I had to do everything. I would drive to the grocery store and sit in the car and cry. He had always done the shopping because I hated it. Once I was shopping and my list disappeared. I caught my breath: *"Oh, I lost my list"* escaped my mouth. Then a voice in the next isle said, *"Would you like to borrow mine?"* So shopping became not so distressing.

Several times in my life I've gone back to school. First I finished my BA and taught Special Ed for a few years. I went back again to study architecture. School was a lot more fun as an adult than as a kid when grades were so important. I was 68 when I last returned to school to learn AutoCad.

Nursing husband for four years, I was pretty much stuck at home, so I learned to make bed and art quilts from books and magazines. Toward the end, Hospice insisted I needed to go back to dancing. A year and a half and four partners later I found my 3rd mate, an elegant ballroom dancer.

I think the most important things I've learned are: *conquer your fears*. Don't let them master you. If you work through them, you'll discover they weren't as bad as you thought. A fellow writer once said to me: *"I see why you are so good at so many things. You keep at them until you get good."* That's the second lesson. The harder something is, the greater your joy in mastering it.

The Voice

By Judy Marie

The degenerative bone condition that started in my childhood about the age of ten caused severe inflammation in my spine. This pain I experienced created a daily struggle, and with each passing year it became more and more intense.

Innumerable health conditions plagued me as a child; from urinary tract infections to chronic constipation, I could not find relief – I only had a bowel movement two to four times a month. By twelve years old, discomfort in my legs made it extremely difficult to walk.

The only solution being offered by doctors was surgery on my L4 disc. A few years later I was in the operating room again, this time to have surgery on the L5 disc and to remove fragments from the first surgery. As a teenager I developed rheumatoid arthritis and sciatica, which accompanied the degenerative bone condition I had.

The year was 1985. I had given birth to my third child
seven months prior to hearing The Voice. By this time,
my lower back and leg pain had progressed. The only
way for me to get out of bed and move up and down
without muscle spasms was by wearing a back brace. At
the age of 28, a mother of three young children, one still
an infant, I found myself in the office of an orthopedic
surgeon, yet again. After reviewing the tests with me he
recommended surgery and explained the pros and cons.

Even though I felt an intense tightening in my gut,
surgery seemed like the logical decision. I thought there
were no other options. I was sitting in the doctor's office
staring at the permission form for yet another back
surgery, when I first heard The Voice. It was
unmistakable when The Voice spoke, saying, *"Judy, no
more!"* and felt undeniable, magnetically vibrating every
cell of my being. A strong sprinkling of angelic dust came
over me.

Divine vapors stirred higher faculties within me that
previously had been dormant. I was plugged into an
awareness of ultimate reality. My spine immediately went

erect in the chair as an illuminating, clear white light permeated all through me. The color of this iridescent energy was a bright white yet I could see through it. My 'mind chatter' was completely shut off. A powerful, loving and direct communication from God, from the Divine, from all that is consciousness engulfed my being.

Instantly, an overwhelming warmth, love, and peace flooded my consciousness. My entire essence was transformed by this ever-flowing magnificent Divine presence. A tingly sensation pulsated throughout my body that affected my hearing and eyesight. My hearing momentarily became disengaged from any earthly tones as if everything was in extreme slow motion. I remember watching the doctor's lips move as he was speaking yet his words were soundless. What I did hear was "nothing." I only sensed a deep vibration of peace.

Next, I automatically removed my glasses because they seemed too strong for my eyes. I realized my eyesight was temporarily restored to perfect vision. The Voice was guiding me away from one place and towards something better. My life's compass changed direction at that moment, and I knew anything was possible. The Voice of Divine Truth and Guidance was unlocked inside me. That day a cosmic ocean of consciousness united waves of knowing, via 'The Voice.' My life cord became plugged into the universal socket of knowing, and was there to stay. This wasn't embarrassing to me, nor did I feel shy about it—I felt completely empowered by The Voice.

As I was driving home, I knew my car was in motion yet I was completely unaware of everything around me. My hearing was still altered and amplified with positive energy. Nothing negative could vibrate in me as if I were in a safe bubble of love and light. I had no worries, no concerns, no anger, resentments, or anxiety—only total peace and love. An overwhelming, peaceful realization swept through me; I was done with surgeries and pain medications forever. To my surprise, I effortlessly stopped taking medications cold turkey. This may not be appropriate in all situations, however in my own, the transition was utterly natural.

There was a new awareness of energy moving through my body, instilling me with hope, help, and healing. My spirit was being steered in an unknown direction yet I completely trusted the force behind it. My world had been jolted for the better, I felt born for the first time. My life as I knew it took a sudden turn where my north became south and my south became north.

Over time I have learned that the experience of pain can lead to great joy, as long as we are open to learn and grow from it. My suffering has not only led to my own personal healing, but it also prepared me to assist many others who are living in physical, emotional, and spiritual distress. I have discovered that we are all connected.

The path of hope and healing is available to everyone. God is ringing the old fashioned dinner bell, telling us it is time to come eat. Vibrations are shaking with change, from drastic and extreme weather conditions to government disturbances, we are transitioning, and ultimately moving from fear into love.

The key is to be open and receptive. When The Voice speaks, you will have no doubt where it comes from and what to do next.

Regardless of how stuck my body was, I simply believed that one day, somehow in time, the purpose behind all my anguish would be revealed. At the core of each experience, no matter how difficult, I discovered a gem containing truth, beauty, and the real me.

Be Brave

By Gayle Dwyer

Too young to be old,
too old to be young.

Be not afraid
Be not afraid
Be not afraid

The limbs a bit weaker,
the bones not quite as strong.

Be not afraid
Be not afraid
Be not afraid

Heads no longer turn upon entering a room,
they barely notice you walking the street.

Be not afraid
Be not afraid
Be not afraid

The list of chores gets longer,
the energy dissipates.

Be not afraid
Be not afraid
Be not afraid

Life as we know it
is changing before our eyes.

Be not afraid
Be not afraid
Be not afraid

Embrace the benefits of aging,
you are wiser than you know.

Be not afraid
Be not afraid
Be not afraid

Enjoy the comfort of wisdom,
and the events that brought you here.

Be not afraid
Be not afraid
Be not afraid

Invest in tomorrow,
and hone your gifts from God.

Be not afraid
Be not afraid
Be not afraid

Yesterday is a memory, tomorrow is yet to come.
Live in the moment fondly, embrace today.

Be grateful
Be hopeful
Be joyful.

Be brave
Be brave
Be brave

Sharing Your Wisdom

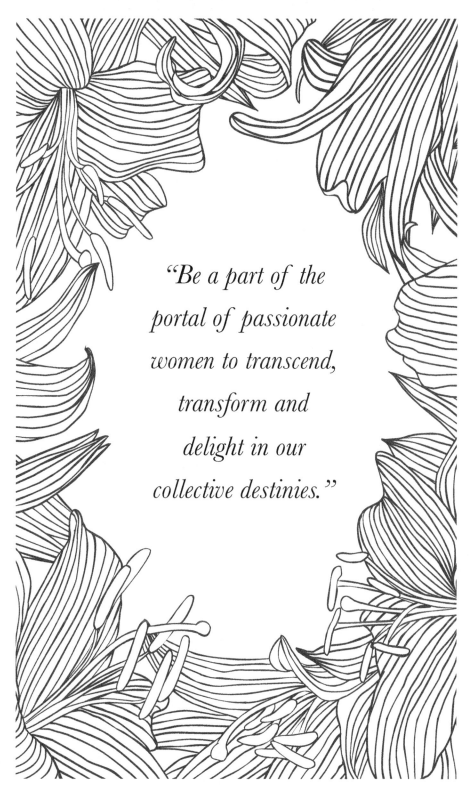

"Be a part of the portal of passionate women to transcend, transform and delight in our collective destinies."

The Power of Sharing

You are honoring the second half of life, and have the opportunity to create a personal one-on-one community to encourage other women to come home to their authentic selves and glow from within!

Women are hungry to share their stories, experiences and wisdom. There is a special sacred connection when women in this passage of life, can sit within a small group and share their journey with the likemindedness of other women who have discovered and are continually discovering themselves.

We are ambassadors of wisdom!
Our voice is valuable!
Share your inner world to the outer world!

People mirror back your evolved growth wisdom as it is a confirmation of the wholeness, or deeper yet… your holyness!

I notice when I pass a woman of experience, there is this wise subtle nod and a look in their eye of being confident with themselves!

Wisdom is life lessons learned!
You can't teach wisdom. The medal of
honor we wear so proudly in our hearts
is something we can only get with
time and discovery.

I am so very excited to share with you how I got started in this magical process!

As a cosmetologist and owner of *Silver~The Organic Salon Retreat,* my services were not limited to just hair – it included personal growth as well! The space was a one-on-one atmosphere of sacred privacy and comfort… my clients got my full attention without all the drama of most salons.

My intention was to draw clientele who were wanting to transition, and to help them with the process of going silver, to become authentic through and through.

As 3 years passed, I met the most incredible women! Through the consultation processes, and as women shared their stories, it became apparent to me, how important the need was to gather women in a confidential, nurturing space.

I then decided to create *"Honoring the Second Half of Life Women's Circle"*. Well, I can tell you, it was fabulous! Our small group enjoyed themselves so much they wanted it to continue! The women looked forward to it every month! The *"Wisdom Connection"* has steadily continued on, and I am so very excited to share the process with YOU!

Knowing that you will be making an amazing difference in people's lives is priceless!

Creating Your own Circle

We are experts at aging because we are living it! As agents of change, we can share our stories and wisdom!

I am encouraging you to look for women who are on the same path as yourself, and the same values and integrity. As we age, spirituality becomes a big part of our lives. We get in touch within the divinity of life.

The circles are to enrich our selves. They are not religious or therapy sessions. Leave that to the professionals. What they hold is the key to self expression and self actualization. Depending on the topic (which I will give you suggestions in a moment) they are to inspire, uplift and educate.

Setting the Tone

Keep it up beat! There will be times where the group takes another road. Allow that to happen! You are the facilitator and can interject as the evening proceeds, to add or if you feel the need to reign the conversation in and want to stay on topic.

Suggested Timing

I suggest a group no more than 12 people. A two-hour timeframe works well, it gives everyone a chance to share. Some people get long-winded and there are times when the story deserves to be heard!

Suggested Topics

AGING GRATEFULLY AND GRACEFULLY:

- Gratitude, peace and harmony of where we are at this very moment
- How we celebrate this passage of life, the sweet spot within our mindful moments of personal growth, ambitions and passions
- The process of reinventing, reigniting our life
- How we discover and re~write our valuable stories

- How do we embrace our human-ness, our authentic selves, feeling comfortable in our own skins, friendships, quality of life?

EMBRACING CHANGE:

- How do we embrace change?
- Do we react or respond?
- How do we do it differently to have a positive outcome for a peaceful experience?
- On the flip side, what strength got you through a transitional time?
- What gave you the courage to make that change in your life?

STORIES OF HEALING:

- How we welcome and integrate the gift of healing stories from others
- How being in nature heals the spirit
- Finding sacred space, "being" in the moment to listen to our intuition

THE REALITY CHECK of our season in life

- Lets get down to the nitty gritty; from our bodies changing, our outlook on the years we have left, to our emotions and how our energies have shifted, we have gained wisdom.
- How do we carry and integrate our inner child/ young girl as we move through our life phases?
- Wish list of things we'd like to experience during this unique transition of life.

OUR DEFINING MOMENTS:

- Reinventing ourselves as we step outside of cultures assumptions about aging, courageously breaking down the walls of stereotypes of how women age while supporting each others individual personal growth and journeys
- How do we live from our mind, body, soul and hearts?
- How we speak and live our truth?

Feel free to use the *Own your Wisdom Creed* on p. 203 for inspirational topics!

Final Thoughts

Acknowledgements

First, I want to thank *You,* the reader, from the bottom of my heart for picking up and reading this book! It is my humble hope that *Own Your Wisdom* has inspired you to tap into the amazing woman you are, and that it guides you to find the deepest voice within and the love of yourself!

Through my life, I had many twists and turns where I lost my footing. In those rocky, uncertain, scary times, I was lifted, carried and cradled by what I call my human angels!

They saw in me what I could not see in myself during my most challenging times. They pushed me out of my comfort zone, held a mirror to my face so I could get a closer peek into my higher self. They believed in me, celebrated, mentored and supported each crossroad with understanding, incredible patience, compassion, kindness, and tough love when I needed it!

They woke me up to my passions, potential and purpose! These amazing people gave me the courage to move forward and awaken with clarity and integrity. I wouldn't be who I am today without my many guides in this world and the grace of the all-knowing Divine!

We are all students and teachers. Each of us has the golden opportunity to shine our unique light of spirit onto the lives around us and the world with the power of love!

My free spirit, out of the box, road less traveled nature has given me the greatest honor and opportunity to meet these wonderful people along my path.

• • •

Lyza Fontana, my get-it-done girl who kept me grounded and focused. This book is in your hands because of her wisdom, creativity, caring, expertise, and the belief in my work and passionate mission.

Tom Bruner, a world traveler, friend and messenger of change.

Jeannie Paulsen, my lifeline and friend who yanked me out of my darkest times with tenacious love and guidance.

Florence Teskey, my accountant who gifted me with her generous heart.

Elaine Voci, my life coach who saw the best in me. She lovingly guided, mentored and believed there was more to myself than my circumstances.

Reid Finch, showed me how to be in love along with his mother Charlotte Yost, a prayer warrior, who opened the door to my spirituality.

To my family, my mother Barbara, my father Norman and sister Patricia.

Adriana Attento, a kindred spirit and new friends in Ventura.

Gregory Reide, my muse and who taught me how to love boldly.

Carolyn Bookout, a constant sparkling jewel in my life.

To the original Honoring the Second Half of Life Women's Circle in Indianapolis, Indiana who continue to inspired and touch my life...

Gail Anderson, Vicki Barlett, Annie Sever-Dimitri, Virginia Biasizzo, Gayle Dwyer, Sharon Mckittrick, Susan Mefford, Jane Parr, Teri Siegel, Meg Summers, Ella Tunnell, Suzi Wagman, Marilyn York, Rosanne Wohlwender. All of these wise women have impacted my life on every level!

To the holistic community in Indy with their contribution of love and healing. Audrey Barron owner of Ezra's Enlightened Cafe, Wendell Fowler nutrition guru, Allie Marie, raw food chef and coach, and so many more dear friends, another book to be written!

The generous clients I was honored to serve who were more than clients, they became long-time friends as well.

To all the dogs and cats in my life with their unconditional love.

My deepest gratitude to all! I love each and every person who has graced my life! They touched my life so I can now touch yours! I look forward to the new people I will meet along my ever-evolving journey to the awakening of self and wisdom! I hope it is you!

With passionate loving kindness and blessings,
Karen Leslie

Suggestions

When inspired and have the courage to go deeper, I suggest re~reading the book using "I" statements, first person in place of we, us, our and so forth. I have done this myself! Powerful inner work!

For instance;
Now is the time in our lives to manifest the true path to our powerful selves!

Using "I" statements;
Now is the time in my life to manifest the true path to my powerful self!

Choose the quotes that speak to you as affirmations!
A great way to start your day with a quote that inspires you to be all that you are, capable, powerful, secure in your wisdom!

You can find more resources and materials at:
www.wisewomenawakened.com

"The summit of my internal wealth will be reflected in my outer life."

Journal Your Wisdom

Writing is a Work of Art

The canvas of lines on paper...

The emphasis of the pen in motion

Delighting in the flow of ink

While writing the lines disappear

The page becomes one with the artists hand

Writing of visions - the image on paper

The storyline that comes from within,

transfers in calligraphy

The sweeps of letters merging in life's flow

Pictures come alive

The writer trying to catch up

with thought on paper...

Magnificent - vibrant - serene

The story never quite ends

The visions explode on the ink trail

The art of writing satisfies the hunger of

the most inner private thoughts...

Thoughtful - satisfying - delicious!

The writing artist

Journal Your Wisdom...

Journal Your Wisdom...

Journal Your Wisdom...

Journal Your Wisdom...

Journal Your Wisdom...

Journal Your Wisdom...

Journal Your Wisdom...

Journal Your Wisdom...

Journal Your Wisdom...

Journal Your Wisdom...

Made in the USA
Las Vegas, NV
01 March 2023

68352529R00184